PUEBLO MAGIC

IN THE LAND OF MONTEZUMA

"The Watch for Montezuma" by Paul Frenzeny and Jules Tavernier as it appeared in *Harper's Weekly* on May 22, 1875.

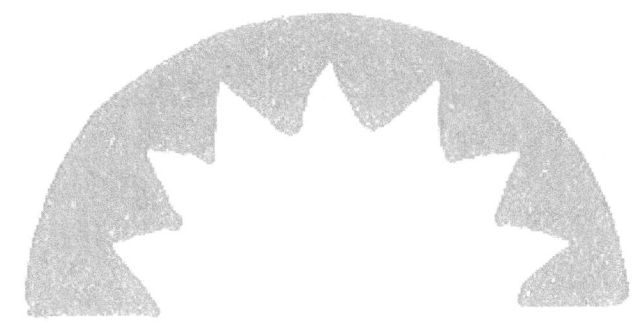

PUEBLO MAGIC
IN THE LAND OF MONTEZUMA

John LeMay

DEAD HORSE HISTORY

A SUBSIDIARY OF BICEP BOOKS. ROSWELL, NEW MEXICO

Printed in the United States of America

LeMay, John.
Pueblo Magic in the Land of Montezuma
ISBN 978-1-953221-14-8
New Mexico/Arizona—Folklore/Anthropology

For Ted Schooley, who grew up in the land of Montezuma, and Marisalena Manchego, who has an appreciation for the mystical

In 1854 the United States purchased a 29,670 square mile portion of Mexico for $10 million as part of the Gadsen Purchase. The newly acquired land was integrated into New Mexico Territory. In 1861, residents of Dona Ana County petitioned to secede from New Mexico Territory. With portions of Franklin County, Texas, Dona Ana wanted to become the seat of a new territory to be called Montezuma Territory. Obviously, this never came to fruition, and the choice of Montezuma as the potential territory's namesake was interesting to say the least.

A NOTE FROM THE AUTHOR

"The land of the Indian is truly the "home of Montezuma." Legend relates that the fires on the mountainsides, lighted one day in seven, are for the second coming of Montezuma. The Indian is always careful to be kind to a stranger, for at one time Montezuma returned in the guise of a beggar; and they turned him away."—Annie Laurie Snorf, Yucca Land: A Collection of the Folklore of New Mexico.

Who is Montezuma? While the obvious answer would be the Emperor of Mexico, in the Southwest region of North America, the name Montezuma belonged to an entirely different entity. Along the same lines, many have puzzled over the names of Montezuma Castle and the nearby Montezuma Well in Arizona since the Aztec emperor never visited either spot. Likewise, Arizona also has three formations known as Montezuma's Head, while New Mexico boasts an entire village named Montezuma, plus its own Montezuma Castle.

So far as anyone knows, Montezuma never made it north of what is today "the Border." So how did the Aztec ruler become synonymous with so many place names and traditions in the Southwest? Basically, through a complicated string of events, Montezuma became conflated with a legendary Pueblo deity from New Mexico and Arizona, which will be explained more thoroughly in the pages ahead.

My introduction to Montezuma in the American Southwest was through the wondrous Pecos Pueblo, with its tales of eternal flames and giant serpents linked to Montezuma. I wrote of both in *The New Mexico Book of Witches*, and this tome actually began as an abridged version of that one, which slanted towards the Spanish Colonial era of New Mexico. But as this title developed, Montezuma slowly took over, and the Montezuma of the Southwest finally had his own book, which has been long overdue.

John LeMay

Table of Contents

INTRODUCTION
In the Land of Montezuma

Histroically, Montezuma is known as the emperor of the Aztecs. The Aztecs had many emperors, of course, but Montezuma is the best-remembered of them being the one that fell to the Spanish conquistadors in 1520. However, in the late 19th and early 20th century, the name Montezuma carried a double meaning across the American Southwest. For instance, you may recall the places names of Montezuma Castle and Montezuma Well in Arizona—two spots the great Aztec emperor certainly never visited. Then there was the odd practice in New Mexico of the Puebloans who watched for Montezuma every sunrise. In that case, Montezuma was thought of as a pueblo messiah of sorts.

In that vein, writers of the early 20th century sometimes called Montezuma the "Moses of the Aztecs" and also their "Nazareth." Those monikers referred neither to the historical Montezuma or even the Aztecs themselves, though. Rather, they referred to a god-man of the pueblos known as Poseyemu, who over time became conflated with Montezuma. Partly to blame for this was the fact that back in the mid-1800s, Anglo settlers wrongly assumed that the indigenous peoples of North America, particularly the Puebloans, were descended from the Aztec. Not only that; they also believed Montezuma was born in the Southwest of North America. However, this was partially due to the Aztecs themselves having claimed to originate in a land to the north.

Portrait of Montezuma, attributed to Antonio Rodriguez (1636-1691).

For instance, *The Kansas City Journal* of October 27, 1880, reported,

> There seems to be no doubt that the Aztecs migrated from some more northern region into Mexico, and the traditions of the present Pueblos, who are believed to be descendants of the original Aztecs, teach that this very spot [New Mexico] was the birth place of Montezuma.

Montezuma's coronation according to the Durán Codex.

How on earth did the Aztec ruler of Mexico become linked to a pueblo deity in North America, though? Some trace the conflation of the two back to the Pueblo Revolt of 1680. The indigenous tribes of New Mexico, subjugated by the Spanish, had heard tales of Montezuma and the fall of the Aztec Empire for many years by then. The leader of the Pueblo Revolt, a shaman called Popé, used that history to his advantage as rumors were spread that he was in communion with Montezuma. In a sense, it truly was to be Montezuma's

Revenge, since Montezuma was advising Popé in his strategies from beyond the grave. At the same time, Popé was also utilizing the story of the Pueblo deity Poseyemu to his advantage, claiming that it was Poseyemu guiding his efforts to expel the Spanish. Regardless of where Popé received his otherworldly aid, the Spanish were effectively driven from New Mexico in August of 1680 and didn't reconquer their kingdom until ten years later.

Depiction of the Battle of Churubusco, Mexico.

Others point to another conflict—the Mexican-American War of the 1840s—as the origin of the Montezuma myth, claiming the Mexican government forged a document stating that Montezuma was born in New Mexico. This, it was hoped, would rally the Puebloans to side with Mexico as opposed to the U.S. Whatever the case, somewhere in this nebulous history between the 1680s and the 1840s, Poseyemu ceased to be, and the mythical Montezuma emerged.

Before delving into the Montezuma of myth, born in New Mexico, let's first recap the Montezuma of history, who most certainly stuck to Mexico. While it is true that the Aztecs claimed they hailed from a land to the north and migrated south, this occurred long before Montezuma was born in 1466. His true name was Motecuhzoma Xocoyotzin, and was also known as Moctezuma II. His reign lasted around seventeen years, from 1503 to 1520. As we all know, it came to an end upon the arrival of Hernán Cortés and the conquistadors. Cautious but friendly with Cortés initially, Montezuma was eventually killed in late June of 1520 as the Spanish sieged Tenochtitlán.[1]

As stated earlier, though the Aztec Empire itself obviously predated Montezuma by many years, according to Pueblo myth, Montezuma was born in current-day New Mexico and from there led the Aztecs south to Mexico. Montezuma was many things to the Puebloans, including prophet, priest, and their first ruler. To some extent, this idea was passed off as fact rather than legend by some early-day sources. For instance, the Chicago *Inter Ocean* of August 22, 1897, stated,

> Montezuma taught them the arts and manufactures which distinguish these tribes from their nomadic brethren of the plains, he gave them the primitive religious ideas which even today exercise a certain influence over their lives, in spite of the Christian ideas which have slowly been introduced among them by the devoted men and women who have passed their lives at these isolated posts of duty and privilege.

A few early-day historians naturally puzzled over Montezuma's "origins" in New Mexico. "No mention is made of Montezuma in Spanish documents on the Southwest of an earlier date than 1664," wrote one of the first great explorers of New Mexico, Adolph Bandelier.[2] Bandelier most likely spoke of Francisco de Gorraez Beaumont and Antonio de Oca Sarmiento's discovery of the ruins of Mexico's Casas Grandes in 1644, which they called the "old houses of Montezuma." Over time, any ancient ruin was given the slang term of a *montezuma*. Even the indigenous peoples of El Paso referred to old ruins as *montezumas*, even though the Aztec ruler probably never crossed what would later be referred to as "the Border."

On the note of Beaumont and Sarmiento's discovery of Casas Grandes, Bandelier observed, "Such an utterance, coming from Spanish officers of high rank, shows that already then the name Montezuma had become, in the minds of the Spaniards themselves, confounded with migration-tales of Indian tribes of a very ancient date."[3]

Likewise, in his *History of Arizona and New Mexico, 1530-1888*, Hubert Howe Bancroft wrote:

> It is also still the custom of most writers to refer to the ruins and relics of this region as undoubtedly of Aztec origin, and to adopt more or less fully the theory that the ancestors of the Pueblo tribes were Aztecs left in Arizona during the famous migration from the north-west to Mexico. As the reader of my *Native Races* is aware, it is my belief that no such general migration occurred, at least not within any period reached by tradition ; but whether this belief is well founded or not, I have found no reason to modify my position that the New Mexican people and culture were not Aztec. The Montezuma myth of the Pueblo communities, so far at least as the name is concerned if not altogether, was certainly of Spanish origin.[4]

Returning to Bandelier, he made a similar summation regarding the Spanish and the Puebloans regarding Montezuma:

> The confusion between those two personages had already been procreative of a mythical Montezuma in the minds of the educated people. Is it to be wondered at if that mythical figure took a still stronger hold on the conceptions of the simple Indian?[5]

The myth of Montezuma as a pueblo messiah was primarily confined to Arizona and New Mexico as opposed to other regions. It was also arguably more prevalent in New Mexico. In *Coronado's Children*, folklorist J. Frank Dobie explained, "Various localities of New Mexico claim to be the birthplace of Montezuma and to be now the repository of his hidden treasures; but the claim of Pecos village is most insistent, most famous."[6]

Postcard depicting the remains of Pecos Pueblo, where Montezuma was once said to rule.

In addition to Pecos, stories circulated that Montezuma was also born either at Taos, Acoma, or at the present-day location of Las Vegas, near the hot springs. However, it was always Pecos Pueblo that Montezuma was most associated with. In short, the story went that Montezuma was a special figure who eventually took the main leadership position at Pecos Pueblo before leaving for Mexico on the wings of a giant eagle. After his departure, Montezuma left the perennial lost treasure in his wake, in addition to a sacred flame burning somewhere either in a mountain cave or on a sun altar. If one found the flame, they might attain immortality and unlimited magical powers. To keep the flame lit, Montezuma entrusted twelve virgin daughters of the pueblo leaders to keep it aflame. If they did so, one day he would return. However, one night one of the girls let the flame extinguish, thus explaining why Montezuma never returned.

This is but one of many examples of the pueblo magic created by Montezuma, and in the pages ahead, many more are about to unfurl…

Section Notes

---

[1] Reports of just how he died and on what day are disputed, but for certain his reign ended around this time. Some say he was stoned by his own subjects on June 29th while Franciscan friar Bernardino de Sahagún claimed that Cortés's forces killed the emperor.

[2] Bandelier, "'Montezuma' of the Pueblo Indians," *American Anthropologist* (Vol.5. October 1892), p.320.

[3] Ibid.

[4] Howe, *History of Arizona and New Mexico*, pp.4-5.

[5] Ibid.

[6] Dobie, *Coronado's Children*, p.204.

PART I

Origins of the Legend

"The Indians here do not know the name Aztec. Montezuma is the outward point in their chronology; and as he is supposed to have lived and reigned for all time preceding his disappearance, so do they speak of every event preceding the Spanish conquest as of the days of Montezuma. The name, at this moment, is as familiar to every Indian, Puebla, Apache and Navajoe as that of our Saviour or Washington is to us. In the person of Montezuma, they unite both qualities of divinity and patriot."— Lieutenant W.H. Emory,
Notes of a Military Reconnaissance from Fort Leavenworth to San Diego, *page 64*

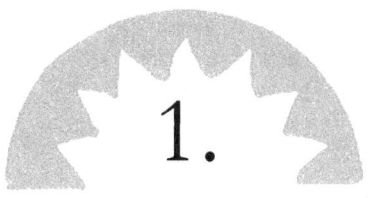

1.

POSEYEMU & MONTEZUMA
The Pueblo Messiah

"All primitive peoples recognize the benefits conferred on them by the sun and are therefore, in the beginning, more or less sun worshipers," began Frank Applegate in his chapter on Montezuma in *Indian Stories from the Pueblos*.[1] And that is essentially what the mythical Montezuma was: a deification of the sun. However, this Montezuma was also a Christ-like figure who came into the world via a virgin birth and was looked upon for many years to one day return. That said, the name Montezuma was not bestowed upon him until later, for originally, he was known as Poseyemu.[2]

As one of Applegate's informants explained it to him, "Pose Ueve, was born without a father like the Christian Jesus, which perhaps made him very unusual."[3] W.E. Curtis, managing editor of the Chicago *Inter-Ocean*, toured New Mexico in the 1880s and was also struck by the story. His impressions of Poseyemu were published in the *Las Vegas Daily Gazette* of April 29, 1883:

> ...the circumstances of his birth and youthhood are strangely similar to those that we read in the New Testament of the days of the child Christ. When he grew to manhood he became their prophet, priest, and king, and ... built a church, at which, according to their traditions, the Aztec religion was born.[4]

It's debatable if the Puebloans added Christ-like attributes to Poseyemu post-conquest/post-Catholicism, but for certain, at his core, Poseyemu was a personification of the sun in superhuman form.[5] The name Poseyemu meant *He who scatters the mists in the morning*, and though commonly attributed to have been born at either Pecos Pueblo or near the hot springs of Las Vegas, more likely he was born at the large pueblo of Pose Uingge, today nothing more than ruins residing twenty miles north of San Juan.

San Juan Mission.

Poseyemu kept to himself as a boy, scorning the other children to wander the wilderness where he conversed with animals and invisible spirits. When the pueblo *cacique*, or medicine man, passed on unexpectedly, lots were drawn to choose the successor. Poseyemu was chosen through this process, much to the chagrin of the older men. Before this, Poseyemu was regarded as something of a simpleton and an outcast. He also dressed the part of one until his "mother and grandmother made him the most beautiful clothes of which they were capable and ornamented them with the sky-colored turquoise," Applegate recorded.[6]

He elaborated that "When Pose Ueve had washed himself and arranged his hair properly, and arrayed himself in his new clothes, everyone was amazed at his handsome appearance and could not believe he was the same Pose Ueve they had always seen so ragged and unkempt."[7]

Pioneer Josiah Gregg, pictured in the portrait above, visited Pecos Pueblo and took note of the legend of Montezuma. Gregg was astute enough to correlate the practices at Pecos with sun worship as Frank Applegate had also done:

> No other Pueblo appears to have adopted this extraordinary superstition: like Pecos, however, they have all held Montezuma to be their perpetual sovereign. It would likewise appear that they all worship the sun; for it is asserted to be their regular practice to turn the face towards the east at sunrise.[8]

Poseyemu soon demonstrated special powers, such as locating abundant game and calling down rain from the heavens to water the crops. In no time, he was revered by all. However, the elders at his pueblo eventually angered him and he traveled south to Pecos Pueblo. There, he chose the new name of Montezuma for himself, and the once small pueblo grew into one of the largest settlements in the region. A vision from the Great Spirit instructed Montezuma to take for himself a wife, Malinche, the daughter of the *cacique* at Zuni Pueblo.[9]

View looking out from the church at Pecos Pueblo. (Author's photo)

For a time, the two ruled like a king and queen to the delight of their subjects. Then, one day, the Great Spirit sent Montezuma a great eagle for he and Malinche to depart upon. Together they flew southward, with new pueblos springing in their wake until finally they arrived at the spot of Tenochtitlán in Mexico. According to the article "La Sierra Glorietta" published on page eight of the *Terre Haut Saturday Evening Mail* of June 21, 1884, the route was as follows:

The first place the Eagle alighted, the city of Santa Fe was founded; the second was where the city of Albuquerque now is, then came Socorro, then El Paso and after a great flight the Eagle at sunrise rested on a Cactus bush and caught a snake. There was founded the city of Mexico and named in honor of Mexitt, the Aztec God of war.

MONTEZUMA'S GOLDEN SHOES

Another variation says that rather than by eagle, Montezuma traveled to Mexico via a pair of golden shoes. These special golden shoes were taken by the Spanish, and as such, Montezuma could not escape back to New Mexico during the conquest. In *A Visit to the Aboriginal Ruins in the Valley of the Rio Pecos*, Adolph Bandelier noted his own curiosity on the subject:

> What the Indians themselves say of this tale I have not as yet ascertained; but the people of the valley all assert that the people of the pueblo believe in it, that they even affirmed that Montezuma was born at Pecos; that he wore golden shoes, and left for Mexico, where, for the sake of these valuable brogans, he was ruthlessly slaughtered. [p.112.]

Upon arriving in Mexico, Montezuma was tempted by the "Evil One" to worship him, which he refused, similar to Christ's forty-day test in the wilderness, where he rebuked the Devil's offers. The rest of the mythical Montezuma's reign in Mexico is somewhat nebulous whereas the Puebloans were concerned. Furthermore, what the Puebloans thought of the real Montezuma's death during the conquest of Mexico is unknown for the most part. But, like Christ's promise to return to Earth one day, the Puebloans had a tradition of looking to the dawn sky for Montezuma's return each day for many years. When he returned, it was thought that he would set the Puebloans free of their oppressors.

Of course, back in those days, history was neither carefully recorded nor easily accessible. Though the Puebloans heard tales of the real Emperor Montezuma to the south, they were unaware that he was not actually the founder of the Aztec empire, but merely its last great overseer before being overthrown by the Spanish.

As stated in the introduction, it is thought that Popé, leader of the Pueblo Revolt, took advantage of the myth of Poseyemu's return in 1680 when the rebellion was in the planning stages. At that time, Poseyemu was just that— Poseyemu. Popé or one of his advisors also decided to throw the great enemy of the Spaniards, that being the deceased Montezuma, into the mix. Due to that, over time, Montezuma and Poseyemu somehow became one and the same.

Chapter Notes

[1] Applegate, *Indian Stories from the Pueblos*, p.116. Applegate got his rendition from a Tewa Indian "of one of the upper Rio Grande pueblos."

[2] Throughout the text you will see numerous alternate spellings of Poseyemu, such as Po-he-yemu, Pose Ueve, and so on.

[3] Applegate, *Indian Stories from the Pueblos*, p.116.

[4] Curtis, "The Pecos Legend," *Las Vegas Daily Gazette* (April 29, 1883).

[5] However, virgin births weren't uncommon in other religious stories and mythologies.

[6] Applegate, *Indian Stories from the Pueblos*, p.116.

[7] Ibid.

[8] Gregg, *Commerce of the Prairies*, p.190.

[9] In all likelihood, Poseyemu taking the name of Montezuma, and also for a wife Malinche, were flourishes added to the tale in the 1840s. See the chapter on Montezuma in the Mexican-American War for more.

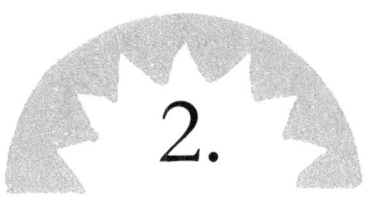

2.

POSEYEMU IN THE PUEBLO REVOLT
Manipulation of Montezuma

In a strange, roundabout way, the Pueblo Revolt of 1630 could be considered the true Montezuma's Revenge.[1] As alluded to several times earlier in this tome, from beyond the grave, Montezuma certainly played a part in the rebellion, which culminated in the city of Santa Fe being seized on Friday the 13th of August in 1680.

The rebellion began on the morning of the 10th when the Puebloans set free the horses of the Spaniards so they could not escape on them and then sealed off the roads leading into Santa Fe. Village by village they began their siege and by the 13th had reached the capital. Santa Fe fell within a week, the Spaniards fled, and in the end, 400 were dead. The Spanish made their way to the safety of El Paso, where they eventually concluded that the Indians only carried out this magnificent feat with the aid of the Devil.

The leader of the revolt was a shaman named Popé, one of 47 medicine men to have been brutally whipped at the behest of the governor in 1675. Popé spent the next five years planning the rebellion. To do so, Popé used the beliefs of the Spanish against them, stating that he was aligned with the Devil. To his own people, though, he claimed to be under the guidance of Poseyemu, and also the long-deceased Aztec emperor, Montezuma.

Perhaps it was no coincidence that Popé was from San Juan Pueblo, since it was said that Poseyemu was born at Pose Uingge, twenty miles north of San Juan. Popé told his followers that at the kiva at Taos, Poseyemu came up from the underworld to commune with him in person. In other versions, rather than Poseyemu himself, it was just an emissary of his.

Taos Pueblo. (Library of Congress)

J. Manuel Espinoza wrote in *The Pueblo Indian Revolt of 1696 and the Franciscan Missions in New Mexico*,

The word was spread that the 'representative' of Poheyemo was very tall and black, with frightful eyes that were large and yellow. The stratagem was to leave it unclear whether or not Popé was Poheyemo's chosen representative or the earthly embodiment of Poheyemo himself.[2]

Before that, Paul Horgan wrote of this emissary in *The Great River* as well. However, Horgan confused Poseyemu with a place rather than as a person or deity:

It was [Popé's] distinction that great powers had been revealed to him. He was able to say that Montezuma, their ancient war god, in his other-kingdom of Po-he-yemu, was gathering all his forces to lead the Indian people in revolt against the Spaniards. Popé was in direct communication with him through three spirits of the underworld who regularly came to him in the kiva and told him what to do.[3]

In addition to Taos Pueblo, Popé also put on a big show at the pueblo of Nambé, where he met with their medicine man, Ahóa, and his followers. Sitting in the darkness of an old kiva, Popé made a supernatural entrance when a "little light came in through the square opening in the center of the roof, where the ladder entered."[4] *Indian Stories from the Pueblos* related that "The stranger stood just at the foot of the ladder, looking upon those seated about the room. As he looked at them, his eyes seemed to give off sparks of fire."[5] Via religious manipulation, Popé claimed that the recent droughts they were experiencing were due to the old gods turning their backs on them. This happened, Popé said, when they had embraced the God of the Spanish. Upon driving the Spanish from their lands, their old gods would return with the rain.

Popé explained that very soon, one early morning as the sun rose, they would storm Santa Fe, drive out the Spanish, and reclaim their land. Popé then took a small bag of sacred corn meal from beneath his blanket and made a large circle out of it at the foot of the kiva's ladder. Next, he withdrew a "strange-looking material from a little bag be carried, and placing it on the ground in the center of the magic circle, set fire to it."[6] After this, "A dense, pungent, thick smoke curled upward and out of the opening in the roof."[7] Popé threw something into the fire which gave a vile odor, likely sulfur. As the smoke began to clear, at the foot of the ladder appeared "two tall, strange and grotesque-looking figures, their heads crowned with owl feathers, the insignia among the Indians of evil and witchcraft."[8] At the sight of the strange beings, the men of Nambé were nearly frightened to death and felt as though "something were crawling under their scalps."[9]

As promised, Popé asked the two spectral figures if they would help to which they affirmed they would. Popé threw the unknown substance into the fire once more and the figures disappeared in another large waft of smoke. The terrified men of Nambé agreed to participate in the revolt.

Eventually, Friday the 13th of August 1680 was chosen as the day of uprising. To communicate the plan, runners were sent to the pueblos carrying knotted ropes to serve as a countdown to the insurrection. However, on August 9, two Tesuque runners, Nicholas Catua and Pedro Omtua, were captured on their way to one of the pueblos. Under torture they confessed that their orders had come from an "Indian who lives a very long way from this kingdom, toward the north, from which region Montezuma came, and who is the lieutenant of Po he yemu; and that this person ordered all the Indians to take part in the treason and rebellion." [10]

A pueblo runner c. 1914 near Taos, by Carl Moon.

Despite the capture of the two runners, Popé's plan was still executed successfully, albeit a few days early. With the help of their otherworldly emissary, Popé and his forces subjugated Santa Fe and drove away the Spanish, who didn't return for a full ten years. Today, it is thought that this spectral emissary was really a flesh and blood man who lived at Taos Pueblo. Most likely, he was a mulatto from New Spain by the name of Diego Naranjo, who was said to be adept at sorcery. Catholic scholar Fray Angelico Chavez was the main proponent who first put forth the theory that Naranjo was Popé's special informant representing/impersonating Poseyemu.

Fray Chavez ended his discourse on Diego Naranjo with a pueblo folktale about Poseyemu that he speculated could have been composed by Naranjo himself shortly before the revolt. In it, Poheyemo and God have a contest which Poheyemo wins. One could interpret this as representing Pope's bold claims that they would extinguish the Holy Trinity of the Catholic Church. The story ended in a similar manner to Montezuma's departure from Pecos Pueblo:

> Before [Poheyemo] left he told the Indians that there wouldn't be any more war between the Indians and anyone. If there were he would come back. He would gather all the Indians in one place and separate the good people from the witches. Then the earth will crack. Then everything will be new again—"when a mule has a baby." [Chavez. "Pohé-yemo's Representative and the Pueblo Revolt." *New Mexico Historical Review* (Vol. 42, #2), p.115.]

As evidence of this theory, Diego had a brother named Pedro, who was interrogated by the Spaniards on a survey mission to New Mexico in 1681 after the revolt. Then 80 years old, Pedro Naranjo said that he was "a great sorcerer who had come down from the upper pueblos to teach his superstitions."[11] It was Pedro who first told of how Popé communed with three spirits by the names of Caudi, Tilini, and Tleume—today linked with Aztec gods associated with fire and water. According to Pedro, these three spirits claimed that they were on their way to a mythical place called Lake Copala, which was near where the Aztecs emerged from the underworld in their creation myth.

That an Indian man would know of Aztec mythology had always been eyebrow-raising for historians. Therefore, it made sense that the Naranjo brothers, thought to be the sons of Spanish slaves, would be fairly well-versed in the history of the Aztecs. It is thought that Diego and Pedro used this lore to their advantage to frighten the Spaniards and, in the process, passed off the Aztec legends to the Puebloans, who began to revere Montezuma.

Some have also wondered if Naranjo, acting as Poseyemu's human emissary, had ideas of becoming the new leader of New Mexico once the Spanish fled. As Fray Angelico Chavez put it, "Either to enjoy personal power, or to avenge himself on the

Europeans who for so long, and sometimes most cruelly, had lorded it over the primitive colored races, or for both reasons, he most cleverly employed the myth of Pohe-yemo to unite the ever-dissident Pueblo Indians for a successful blow."[12]

Statue of Popé created by Cliff Fragua.

Whatever the case, the ultimate fate of both Naranjo brothers is unknown, and if either had ideas of ruling New Mexico after the Spanish fled, these dreams never came to fruition. Actually, neither did Popé's. Despite Popé's claims, the old gods didn't return to bring the rain and the droughts persisted. The raids by the Navajo and Apache, who had not taken part in the revolt, not only continued but became worse without the Spaniards there. Popé only lasted as the new leader of the Puebloans for nary a year before he dropped out of the history books, never to be seen again. Many have since theorized that he died in 1688, a little before the Spanish reconquest of 1692.[13]

This image, created in 1898, is sometimes described as depicting the Pueblo Revolt, and at other times as Coronado conquering Zuni Pueblo. In either case, it is a famous depiction of violence between the Spanish and the Puebloans.

Ralph E. Twitchell wrote of Pecos in the *Santa Fe New Mexican* of October 27, 1910. Twitchell referred to the legend of Montezuma at Pecos as "the veriest rot," however, and asserted that prior to 1680 the legend of Montezuma at Pecos was nonexistent. He furthermore wondered if, instead, the story of Montezuma was confused for Coronado's promise to return to Pecos after searching out the Seven Cities of Gold. [14]

Ultimately, one could argue that Naranjo brought tales of Montezuma and the Aztecs to the table, while Popé brought that of Poseyemu. The two figures were not yet conjoined though. As Adolf Bandelier surmised, "The [Puebloans of the revolt] treated of Pose-yemo and Montezuma as of two distinct personages though related. In this century they have gradually become confounded."[15]

Chapter Notes

---

[1] Throughout the 20th century, Montezuma's Revenge was crude slang for an upset stomach due to spicy Mexican dishes.

[2] Espinoza, *Pueblo Indian Revolt of 1696*, p.33.

[3] Horgan, *Great River*, p.271.

[4] Applegate, *Indian Stories from the Pueblos*, p.71.

[5] Ibid.

[6] Ibid, p.72.

[7] Ibid.

[8] Ibid.

[9] Ibid.

[10] Hackett and Shelby, *Revolt of the Pueblo Indians of New Mexico*, pp.15-16.

[11] Chavez, "Pohé-yemo's Representative and the Pueblo Revolt," *New Mexico Historical Review* (Vol. 42, #2), p.99.

[12] Ibid, p.89.

[13] Recently a statue was erected of Popé in Washington D.C. However, despite a desire among some to make him out to be a hero, New Mexican historian Ray John De Aragón shed a different light on Popé that others were reluctant to acknowledge. In *New Mexico Native American Lore*, Aragón explained atrocities committed by Popé against his own people who refused to renounce Catholicism. Even worse was his treatment of Spanish families left behind, namely the killing, rape, enslavement and a few instances of ritual sacrifice of young Spanish girls. Among those abused and captured were Aragón's ancestor, Juana de Arzate. Family tradition held that the five-year-old girl watched as Popé's men raped her mother, then beheaded her and her father. The girl remained a slave until the Spanish reconquest of 1692. While the greedy Spanish were no angels, neither were Popé and some of his followers.

[14] For context, Coronado passed through Pecos on his way to the mythical golden city of Quivira and promised to return. In its entirety, Twitchell's quote read: "It may be taken as conclusive that there is no truth whatever in the legend that when Montezuma left the pueblo and went south he commanded that the holy fire should be kept burning t'ill he should return. That the sacred fire had originally nothing at all to do with the Montezuma legend is affirmatively determined by the earliest reports. It is believed that the whole story refers to the presence of Coronado at the pueblo and his promise to return."

[15] Bandelier, "'Montezuma' of the Pueblo Indians," *American Anthropologist* (Vol.5. October 1892), p.322.

"Conquest of New Mexico," engraving of General Kearny
proclaiming New Mexico part of the United States
at Las Vegas on August 15, 1846.

3.

MONTEZUMA IN THE MEXICAN-AMERICAN WAR

Montezuma and Poseyemu in Propaganda

Though the Pueblo Revolt started the process of melding Montezuma with Poseyemu, the two figures would not become permanently conjoined until the Mexican-American War nearly two hundred years later. In what constituted one of the stranger tactics of the war, the Mexican government forged a document implying that the Aztec emperor Montezuma had been born in New Mexico. This undoubtedly stemmed from the much earlier Pueblo Revolt, where tales of Poseyemu and Montezuma being manipulated from beyond the grave were repeated by the survivors. The Mexican government wondered if Montezuma had effectively been used to sway the Puebloans in the past, could he not be exploited again?

As it was, Mexico was no longer New Spain ruled by the Spaniards. Mexico had won its independence in August of 1821. Not only that, much of its population was no longer purely Spanish but was mixed between the Spaniards and the indigenous peoples. It was hoped that perhaps the Puebloans of New Mexico might side with Mexico in the war against the United States. As a way of linking the Puebloans to the people of Mexico, a document entitled "History of Montezuma" was created. What exactly it espoused is unknown, as no copies remain in existence.

Doña Marina (La Malinche) from *The Mastering of Mexico* by Kate Stephens, 1916.

Historians like Adolf Bandelier spoke of this document, though, with Bandelier specifically claiming that it was never widely printed. According to him, it began with the folktale of Poseyemu being born in New Mexico and taking the name of Montezuma at a later date. After this, he flew south on the back of a giant eagle, where he founded the Aztec Empire and, thus, Mexico itself. Again, the purpose of the document was to create a sense of loyalty between the Puebloans and the people of Mexico.

To further that end, the character of Malinche was also added into the mix. Also known as Doña Marina and Malintzin, Malinche was Hernán Cortés's translator during the conquest, and a traitor to her people in the minds of many. She was also the first indigenous person to couple with a conquistador, in this case Cortés, producing the first true *mestizo*.

The forged document made Malinche the daughter of Montezuma when, in fact, she wasn't even Aztec—she was Nahua. The fictional document, in a further effort to bridge the divide between the Puebloans and the Mexicans, claimed that Montezuma gave Malinche away in marriage to Cortés and "representing New Mexico as a part of the dower which the Indian maiden brought to her Spanish husband," according to Bandelier.

Bandelier continued,

> Such a document, manufactured at a time when an American invasion of New Mexico was apprehended, written at the City of Mexico and circulated in every New Mexican pueblo that could be reached, is plainly what may be called a "campaign document," conceived in view of strengthening the claims of Mexico upon New Mexico in the eyes of the Pueblo Indians and refuting anything to the contrary that might be anticipated from the side of the United States. It is written in a peculiarly within the grasp of the Indian, it being Spanish after fashion in which the Pueblo Indian uses that language in conversation.[1]

This document was also alluded to in the *Las Vegas Gazette* of June 20, 1874, and summarized in the following way:

> It is supposed that Montezuma was not the original name of this demi-god, but one bestowed on him after he had proved the divinity of his mission. A document is now extant purporting to be copied from one of the legends at the capitol of Mexico, in which it is stated that Montezuma was born in "Teguayo," one of the ancient pueblos of New Mexico, in the year 1538.

The article went on to assert that this may have been a descendant of the real Emperor Montezuma, one who became "more of a prophet than anything else." The article claimed he "foretold events that actually came to pass," and it was "related of him that he performed many wonderful things."

Back to Bandelier, he noted that the document most likely came from Mexico, but that it was not "impossible that it was a product of New Mexican ingenuity."[2] In 1838, the last residents of Pecos Pueblo, closely associated with Montezuma, migrated to Jemez Pueblo. With them they allegedly took an ancient book entitled "History of the Pueblos."

"I never succeeded in seeing ["History of the Pueblos"], but the Most Reverend Archbishop of Santa Fe, during one of his official visits to Jemez, obtained permission to peruse the mysterious volume," Bandelier stated.[3] In Bandelier's opinion, the "History of Montezuma" may well have been constructed by use of "History of the Pueblos," which contained the account of Poseyemu. Bandelier was of the fascinating opinion that shamans and medicine men gladly repeated the tale of Montezuma to Spaniards and Anglos as a way of keeping the real hero-god of Poseyemu a secret.

To reiterate, this is but one of several theories attempting to explain the nebulous connection between Montezuma and Poseyemu. However the "History of Montezuma" document came about, it didn't help the Mexican effort to win the war, which it had lost by 1848. In the aftermath of the Mexican-American War, a great many tales of Montezuma were picked up by Anglo settlers, particularly those who explored the abandoned ruins of Pecos Pueblo. By then, there was rarely any mention of Poseyemu, who was now firmly known as Montezuma.

Chapter Notes

[1] Bandelier, "'Montezuma' of the Pueblo Indians," *American Anthropologist* (Vol.5. October 1892), pp.323-324.
[2] Ibid, p.324.
[3] Ibid.

PART II

Montezuma at Pecos

"*A tradition was prevalent among them that Montezuma had kindled a holy fire and... that [one day] Montezuma would appear with the sun... .the deluded Indians were to be seen every clear morning upon the terraced roofs of their houses, attentively watching for the appearance of the 'king of light,' in hopes of seeing him 'cheek by jowl' with their immortal sovereign." —Josiah Gregg,* Commerce of the Prairies, *pages 188-189*

4.

CHURCH OF PECOS
Monument to Montezuma

Though several monuments bear his name, two of which go by that of Montezuma Castle, it is probably the ruins of Pecos Pueblo that serve as the place most associated with Montezuma. Ralph E. Twitchell wrote of Pecos in the *Santa Fe New Mexican* of October 27, 1910, calling it the "most interesting ruin in the Southwest."

Located southeast of Santa Fe and southwest of Las Vegas, Pecos Pueblo was established around 1350 A.D. and boasted a population of about 2,000 residents, making it one of the largest pueblos in the region. When Francisco Vázquez de Coronado came across it on his march towards the Seven Cities of Gold, it was called Cicuye by the Spaniards. (To native speakers, it was P`ae'xilâ, though, meaning "the place above the water.") At Cicuye, Coronado and his men met a trickster called "the Turk," who ingeniously led the Spaniards all the way to Salinas, Kansas, in search of the Seven Cities of Gold. Thus, Cicuye managed to peacefully get rid of the Spaniards... for a time at least.

Of course, the Spanish eventually returned and conquered Cicuye like they did all the other pueblos and began construction of a huge church in the 1620s. Its full title was the Mission Nuestra Señora de los Ángeles de Porciúncula de los Pecos.

Ralph E. Twitchell wrote of Pecos in the *Santa Fe New Mexican* of October 27, 1910, and gave the most detailed description of the church:

> A wide circular depression strikes the eye; beyond, flat mounds covered with scattered and broken stones; further, distinct foundations, rectangles enclosed by or originally founded upon thick walls of stone; immediately to the north, more broken walls of stone, and above them all, on a broad terrace of bright red earth, completely shutting off the site of the old pueblo dwellings may be seen what is left of the ancient Catholic; mission of Pecos.
>
> The building was a rectangle, originally about one hundred and fifty feet in length from east to west and about sixty feet from north to south. The entrance was to the west, the eastern wall still standing in part. Twenty-five years ago the gateways were capped by heavy lintels of hewn cedar. These long since have been carried away by the vandal and the relic hunter.
>
> As late as 1858 the roof was still upon the building. The church was probably about thirty-five feet high. According to tradition it had but one belfry and a single bell, but a very large one. The Indians from the pueblo of San Cristoval in 1180 carried it off, so it is said, to the top of the mesa, where it was broken. A portion of this old bell was seen by me once at Pecos town. What has become of it I do not know. Koslowski was the man who took down the roof of the old church, he used the timbers in building outhouses for his ranch nearby. He also attempted to dig out the corner stone, but failed.
>
> In general the vandalism committed since the American occupation of New Mexico upon this ancient relic of antiquity defies all description. All the old beams of the church were quaintly carved. This fact is mentioned by the topographical engineer of the army of occupation in 1846. That the old church has not entirely disappeared, being carried off adobe by adobe, is a mystery.
>
> There has been some speculation as to the age of the old church at Pecos. It is certain that the church was not built at any time within the sixteenth century. It was in all probability constructed some time after 1629. This church was said to be the finest in New Mexico at that time, twenty-six different churches and convents having been built by the Franciscans subsequent to the report made by Zarate-Salmeron. The city of Santa Fe in 1667 had only two hundred and fifty inhabitants, while Pecos, at that time of the Indian uprising of 1680, had more than two thousand.

Pueblo Magic

In 1680, after the Spanish were expelled during the Pueblo Revolt, the people of Pecos built a kiva in front of the church as a way of rejecting the faith of the Spanish. After the reconquest of New Mexico, another smaller church was built in 1717. By the mid-1800s, the population had dwindled to such an extent that the pueblo had to be abandoned completely. The main reason for the depopulation of Pecos was disease introduced by the Spaniards, coupled with Comanche raids. In August of 1838, twenty-one survivors of the once great pueblo migrated to Jemez Pueblo, where they were welcomed due to both pueblos sharing a common lineage.

Having been deserted a decade before the Mexican-American War, the ruins of Pecos Pueblo were especially enigmatic for Anglo settlers and explorers. For instance, the main ruin was called the "Astek Church" by artist John Mix Stanley in 1846, when he sketched the pueblo.

Pecos Pueblo church by Heinrich Balduin Möllhausen (1858).
Note the rather ominous flock of birds hovering over it.

That same year came another intriguing first-hand account, which was published in various newspapers.[1] The author was identified only as E.T.F., said by the paper to be a "son of one of our citizens now on a trading expedition to Zacatecas." His letter was dated and addressed as "Pecos, New Mexico, Oct.

14, 1846." It, too, offered another variation on area legend, likely due to mistranslations and details that became jumbled in translation. For instance, the author noted how the "temple," or Pecos Church, contained "the bones of the descendants of Montezuma." Basically, the way he understood the legend was the opposite of the usual. Instead of Montezuma originating at Pecos, it was Montezuma's royal family who came and built Pecos Pueblo after his death during the conquest of Mexico.

Lt. W.H. Emory's sketch of church at Pecos plus his description:

The accompanying sketches will give a much more accurate representation of these ruins than any written descriptions. The remains of the modern church, with its crosses, its cells, its dark, mysterious corners and niches, differ-but little from those of the present day in New Mexico.

Along these same lines, another legend of the church was related by a private in the army, Josiah M. Rice, who passed through Pecos in 1851 with Colonel Edwin V. Sumner. Rice recorded,

There are many traditions connected with this old church, one of which is that it was built by a race of giants, fifty feet in height. But these, dying off, they were succeeded by dwarfs, with red heads who, being in their turn exterminated, were followed by the Aztecs.

The year 1846 was apparently a busy one at Pecos, for it was explored again by Lieutenant W.H. Emory in the aftermath of the Gadsen Purchase. In his journal, later published as the book *Notes of a Military Reconnaissance from Fort Leavenworth to San Diego*, Emory wrote of Pecos for his entry on August 17th, 1846. Specifically, he honed in on the juxtaposition of the religion of Montezuma intermingling with Catholicism:

Pecos, once a fortified town, is built on a promontory or rock, somewhat in the shape of a foot. Here burned, until within seven years the eternal fires of Montezuma, and the remains of the architecture exhibit, in a prominent manner, the engraftment of the Catholic church upon the ancient religion of the country. At one end of the short spur forming the terminus of the promontory, are the remains of the estuffa, with all its parts distinct; at the other are the remains of the Catholic church, both showing the distinctive marks and emblems of the two religions. The fires from the estuffa burned and sent their incense through the same altars from which was preached the doctrine of Christ. Two religions so utterly different in theory, were here, as in all Mexico, blended in harmonious practice until about a century since, when the town was sacked by a band of Indians.[2]

Luckily, the area was turned into a national monument in 1935, one hundred years after its abandonment, and is carefully kept up as a part of the National Parks System. To this day, the old church still stands as the centerpiece of the monument.

Chapter Notes

---

[1] The letter as published in the *Indianapolis Indiana State Journal* of December 8, 1846, was the source in this instance.

[2] Emory, *Notes of a Military Reconnaissance*, p.30.

Xiuhtecuhtli in the Codex Borgia.

5.

MONTEZUMA'S FIRE
Eternal Flame of Pecos

Before departing Pecos, Montezuma left behind a great treasure, not of gold or silver, but of an eternal flame. A few thought that the eternal flame might grant immortality, but most agreed it existed as a symbol of Montezuma's impending return. Whatever its purpose, it was easily the most famous of Pecos's many legends connecting to Montezuma. So the story went, before departing Pecos, Montezuma lit a sacred fire on a sun altar and commanded that it be fed and kept burning continuously, day and night, by twelve virgin daughters of the pueblo leaders.[1] As long as the fire was kept burning, Pecos would prosper, and in due time, Montezuma would return to resume his reign. According to various stories, the flame either was extinguished out of carelessness or was transferred to another pueblo upon the abandonment of Pecos.

As stated before, exactly what the eternal flame of Montezuma was meant to represent at Pecos is unknown. Zoroastrians worshiped eternal "Pillars of Fire" in their belief system, for instance, and to this day, symbolic eternal flames are used to commemorate events. Sometimes, eternal flames could represent the spiritual presence of a deity. Along those lines, a small fire was permanently kept alive at the sacred center of every Aztec home in honor of Xiuhtecuhtli, the god of fire. The Aztecs believed that if the fire created by

Xiuhtecuhtli died, the entire universe would collapse. If the fire at Pecos was in some way related to this is anyone's guess. A few pioneers were at least aware of the connection between the eternal flame and Aztec customs. W.E. Curtis made the comment in the *Las Vegas Daily Gazette* of April 29, 1883, that "The Aztecs worshiped fire, and Montezuma's principal business when he grew to manhood was to keep the flames upon the hideous old altar [at Pecos] alive."[2]

Sketch of Pecos ruins by Lt. W.H. Emory.

Whatever it represented, the eternal flame was no myth, and a few Anglo explorers attested to have seen it. The most notable of these was Josiah Gregg, who wrote of it in *Commerce of the Prairies*:

I have myself descended into the famous *estujas*, or subterranean vaults, of which there were several in the village, and have beheld this consecrated fire, silently smouldering under a covering of ashes, in the basin of a small altar. Some say that they never lost hope in the final coming of Montezuma until, by some accident or other, or a lack of a sufficiency of warriors to watch it, the fire became extinguished; and that it was this catastrophe that induced them to abandon their villages, as I have before observed.[3]

ANCIENT PUEBLO OF PECOS

Interesting Ruin Twenty Miles Southeast of the City of Santa Fe

FINALLY ABANDONED IN 1840

Took With Them to Jemez the Sacred Fire That Had Burned for Centuries.

In addition to Gregg, a few other Anglos had seen the flame, despite a tradition that Montezuma commanded that no Mexican nor any Anglo was ever to lay eyes on the sacred flame. The author of an article in the *Miami Helmet* of May 27, 1875, recollected that the people of Pecos "valiantly resisted every attempt made by the Mexicans to enter the *estufas*, and I was assured by them that no Mexican had ever seen the inside of one." The author continued,

> I saw and conversed with Americans at Santa Fe who had seen this sacred fire, silently smoldering beneath the ashes upon the altar in this temple, which fire the Aztecs declared had been kept burning for more than four

hundred years without once becoming extinguished. It was tended by the warriors of the pueblo, who, two at a time, maintained their watch for two successive days and nights, during which they were allowed neither food, water or sleep. They were clothed in white robes of cotton, reaching to their feet, and were not permitted to converse during the watch.

Adolph Bandelier heard tales of the flame and its custodians from Mariano Ruíz, who had been among those to leave in the 1838 exodus. In telling Bandelier of the Pueblo's history in 1880, Ruíz said the sacred flame was kept in "a sort of closed oven" and was not actually "permitted to flame."

According to Ruíz, once a year, the Pecos people elected one member of the tribe to tend to the sacred fire.[4] Ruíz said he was relieved that he was never chosen for the deed, as he heard that anyone who left the tribe after attending the fire would die. Ruíz, it should be noted, was not a native of Pecos Pueblo and had been adopted by them.

As stated before, the eternal flame wasn't so eternal and was eventually extinguished. Though most oral histories had the flame dying out, conflicting accounts alleged it was arduously and carefully moved to another location. In *A Visit to the Aboriginal Ruins in the Valley of the Rio Pecos*, Adolph Bandelier heard that "the sacred embers were kept aglow till 1840, and then transferred to Jemez," for instance.[5]

Contrary to the flame being moved, a son of the last living Pecos Indian gave Frank Applegate this account in *Indian Stories from the Pueblos*:

This sacred fire was kept alive and ceremonies were held yearly in honor of Montezuma for many centuries. But one night the twelve virgins, made drowsy by the heat of the fire, fell asleep, and the sacred flame died and the altar became cold.

For their negligence the virgins were punished, disgraced and made outcasts, but from that time the prosperity of the pueblo quickly diminished, and the population declined so much that the head men of Pecos came to the conclusion that the pueblo was accursed because the sacred fire had gone out, and decided to abandon Pecos and go and live with their kinsmen at Jemez, a pueblo which Montezuma had founded with the overflow of population from Pecos, and where yearly their descendants still perform some of the ceremonies brought from the home of their fathers.[6]

General William H. Emory c.1865.

Lieutenant W.H. Emory wrote how the flame was kept lit even amidst attacks from a roving tribe in his 1846 journal. In fact, according to Emory, the flame was still going and had not been extinguished at the time of his exploration in 1846:

Amidst the havoc of plunder of the city, the faithful Indian managed to keep his fire burning in the estuffa; and it was continued till a few years since—the tribe became almost extinct. Their devotions rapidly diminished their numbers, until they became so few as to be unable to keep their immense estuffa (forty feet in diameter) replenished, when they abandoned the place and joined a tribe of the original race over the mountains, about sixty miles south. There it is said, to this day they keep up their fire, which has never yet been extinguished. The labor, watchfulness, and exposure to heat consequent on this practice of their faith, is fast reducing this remnant of the Montezuma race; and a few years will, in all probability, see the last of this interesting people.

The same year that Lieutenant Emory made his observations, an author identified as E.T.F. had a letter dated October 14, 1846, published in the *Las Vegas Gazette* relating details of the eternal flame. His was one of the only accounts that spoke of sacred fires plural. E.T.F. claimed that the flame had been rekindled elsewhere and also that Governor Armijo had something to do with the pueblo being abandoned:

In the grand plaza they dug three deep cisterns; these all communicated with each other by an underground passage. In these cisterns they kindled fires which never went out for more than 300 years, indulging the vain superstition that Montezuma would again visit them before the flame expired. (It was only 10 years ago that Governor Armijo put a stop to their devotions, and caused the flame to be extinguished.) ... But disease and the wild mountain tribe of the [sic] Apachas have lopped off all their royal scions, save two, and these have gone far beyond the Rio del Norte, rekindled again the flame, over which will expire in a few short years, the last of the Montezumas.

It was alleged that General Kit Carson was allowed to observe one of the ceremonies within an estufa. In that case, it was said the celebrants danced around the altar of fire.

One of the wilder fates for the eternal flame went that Montezuma himself returned to collect it. The *Kansas City Journal* of October 27, 1880, noted how the Pecos peoples felt that Montezuma would actually "descend by the column of smoke which rose from the sacred fire." In the pueblo's final days, "three warriors took the remains of the fire and carried it into the mountains, where Montezuma himself appeared and received it." A later letter, dated October 4, 1883, out of Las Vegas, repeated the story in greater detail:

> In 1837 the tribe was reduced to 15 persons, of whom but seven were warriors. All this time they had kept the sacred fire burning, but they could do it no longer, as they were too few, and tradition says that three warriors went into the woods with the fire and that Montezuma himself appeared and relieved them of it. Then they packed their goods and went to join their brothers at the Jemez Pueblo, west of the Rio Grande.[7]

A few years before, the *Kansas City Journal* of July 10, 1881, claimed that the sacred flame had been removed to Taos:

> The sacred fire was kept faithfully burning until about the time of the revolution of 1837,[8] when it was removed with great pomp to Taos, where it is supposed to be still burning, although it is so closely guarded no one but those belonging to the faith are permitted to see it.

The most dramatic account the eternal flame's ultimate fate appropriately came from roving journalist Matthew C. Field, who was also an actor. In 1839, Field spent the night in the only recently abandoned Pecos Church. At the church, Field said that he was entertained by an ancient, stooped over sheep herder with "long silken hair" that was as white as "the snow of 90 winters."[9] From him, he heard a romantic account of the abandonment of Pecos that read like a Greek tragedy when Field recounted it.

The old man's story went that in the last days of Pecos, a "pestilential disorder came ... and swept away the people."

The sacred flame, according to him, resided in "a deep cavern, whose mouth yawns in the hillside behind the church" and by that time "the side of the mountain grew bare as year after year the trees were torn away to feed the consuming torch of Montezuma." Eventually only the chief of Pecos remained alive along with his daughter, Gualupeta, and her betrothed, a young warrior named Josenacio. The old man died, and so Gualupeta and Josenacio went to the hidden cave and retrieved the sacred fire via a brand, which they carried with them outside into the wilderness:

> A light then rose in the sky which was not the light of morning, but the heavens were red with the flames that roared and crackled up the mountainside. And the lovers lay in each other's arms, kissing death from each other's lips, and smiling to see the fire of Montezuma mounting up to heaven.
>
> That summer passed away, and the winter, and when again the grass was green around the desolate city, two skeletons were found mouldering at the mouth of the cavern. These were Gualupeta and Josenacio, the betrothed lovers, the last watchers at the now extinct fire of Montezuma.[10]

After hearing the story, Field claimed that the old man produced a small clay bowl full of burned cinders along with an old burnt stick, which he claimed was actually the remains of the sacred fire. Furthermore, Field even pocketed a few ashes of the sacred fire before departing for San Miguel. Field wrote:

> He took from a niche in the wall a small burnt stick and a little clay bowl full of cinders, which he said he had himself brought from the bottom of the sacred cavern. That these were actually as he said remnants of the sacred fire there is not the slightest doubt, for from after enquiries we found the history he gave us fully confirmed, and the same story was current among all the Americans residing in Santa Fé.[11]

If Field made the account up entirely on his own, or if he really was repeating the tale of a white-haired sheepherder at Pecos, is uncertain. But considering Field's flair for the dramatic, the former is the more likely explanation. In any case, stories of the eternal flame have certainly kept the legend of Pecos Pueblo burning bright.

Chapter Notes

[1] The *Las Vegas Gazette* of June 20,1874, attested that the twelve virgins were selected annually and were not permanent attendants of the flame. Contrary to this, the *Santa Fe New Mexican* of July 21, 1916, reported that Tax Commissioner Amado Chaves obtained a deposition from Jemez from the last survivor at Pecos, stating that it was precisely eight men selected annually for the duty of watching the flame. The piece reported, "Quite often one or more of the eight died and the survivors would come up on New Year's day, weak and tottering, and were led in a procession about the pueblo."

[2] Curtis, "The Pecos Legend," *Las Vegas Daily Gazette* (April 29, 1883).

[3] Gregg, *Commerce of the Prairies*, pp.57-58.

[4] And also the giant serpent that it kept at bay, for that see the following chapter.

[5] Bandelier, *A Visit to the Aboriginal Ruins in the Valley of the Rio Pecos*, p.112.

[6] Applegate, *Indian Stories from the Pueblos*, p.119.

[7] Ibid.

[8] What they called "the revolution" presumably referred to the Mexican American War, which didn't occur until ten years later.

[9] *Matt Field on the Santa Fe Trail*, p.248.

[10] Ibid, p.249.

[11] Ibid, p.251.

6.

MONTEZUMA'S SERPENT
Giant Rattlesnake or Mythical Monster?

Second to tales of the sacred flame were rumors of a giant serpent at Pecos Pueblo. Some accounts held that it was quasi-benevolent, while other renditions made it out to be a monster that demanded human sacrifice. Sometimes, it was portrayed as an articulate, intelligent deity, not unlike the serpentine Quetzalcoatl, while in other accounts, it was simply a gigantic rattlesnake that was symbolic more than supernatural. Whatever its true nature and proportions, the stories went that somewhere inside a mountain cave, the tribe of Pecos kept a giant snake. Often times it was confined by means of a large fire, and occasionally that fire was synonymous with the sacred flame. Considering that stories of the serpent were spread by Anglo and Mexican settlers rather than the Pecos peoples themselves, a great deal of confusion shrouds the truth of the snake.

The mythology of Mesoamerica held a belief in feathered serpents like Quetzalcoatl, while the stories of Native American tribes across North America told of horned serpents, like Awanyu, often associated with water in some way. The serpent at Pecos was different, though, as it was said to be a literal gigantic rattlesnake. And what's more, a few settlers even asserted to have seen evidence of it in the nineteenth century.

Perhaps due to Pecos Pueblo's association with Montezuma, the giant snake was sometimes associated with Quetzalcoatl. *The Santa Fe New Mexican* covered the giant serpent on November 27, 1966, mentioning it in relation to a folk pageant entitled "The Plumed Serpent." The article identified the giant snake as an "enormous, fantastically plumed serpent which was housed in one of the kivas." It also noted that the play "involves the incident of [infant] sacrifice which turned the benevolent yet powerful serpent into the destructive force that drove the Indians from their homes and left Pecos in the state of ruin in which it is seen today."

Supposedly, the snake was so large that it was capable of swallowing a human being whole. Rumors circulated that the tribe's elderly were fed to the monster, as were infants at certain times as a ritual sacrifice. Other accounts claimed that the giant snake was fed fresh game from hunters rather than human beings, while others pointed out that there has never existed a rattlesnake large enough to devour a human to begin with. However, this was no ordinary snake, it was magical. And so the legend goes, when the mystical serpent either left or died, so did Pecos Pueblo. That, they say, is the real reason that in 1838 the last of the pueblo's dwindling population left for Jemez Pueblo.

It was most likely writer Willa Cather who brought the legend to a wide audience when she utilized it in her novel *Death Comes for the Archbishop*, which featured a scene where a priest stays the night in the sacred cave.

Cather wrote:

> There was also the snake story, reported by the early explorers, both Spanish and American, and believed ever since: that this tribe was peculiarly addicted to snake worship, that they kept rattlesnakes concealed in their houses, and somewhere in the mountain guarded an enormous serpent which they brought to the pueblo for certain feasts. It was said that they sacrificed young babies to the great snake, and thus diminished their numbers.

It was in the aftermath of this abandonment that secondhand tales of the serpent began to surface. And, as with tales of the sacred flame, Josiah Gregg was one of the first to report the serpent in *Commerce of the Prairies*. Specifically, Gregg wrote of the snake in association with the tending of the sacred flame, which Gregg explained was overseen by the warriors rather than Pueblo virgins. Gregg said that they would keep watch for two days straight "without partaking of either food, water, or sleep..."[1] Contrary to this, Gregg said that other accounts held that the warriors watched it until the point of starvation. This is where the serpent finally came in, with Gregg recording:

> A large portion of those who came out alive were generally so completely prostrated by the want of repose and the inhalation of carbonic gas that they very soon died; when, as the vulgar story asseverates, their remains were carried to the den of a monstrous serpent, which kept itself in excellent condition by feeding upon these delicacies. This huge snake (invented no doubt by the lovers of the marvellous to account for the constant

disappearance of the Indians) was represented as the idol which they worshipped, and as subsisting entirely upon the flesh of his devotees: live infants, however, seemed to suit his palate best.[2]

Rat-tle-snake.

Along these same lines, a later letter dated October 4, 1883, out of Las Vegas, NM, stated similarly to Gregg that:

Warriors watched the fires and remained on duty for two days and nights without food or rest, or, as, some say, until exhausted or dead; and many that came out alive died soon after. The Spanish Mexicans used to believe that the bodies were given to an enormous serpent to devour.[3]

The letter from Pecos dated October 14, 1846, by the informant identified as E.T.F. also detailed the giant snake:

> Only a peculiar kind of person was permitted to feed this fire, for they supposed if any one of the "Profanum valgus" descended into the cistern, he would be immediately swallowed by an immense serpent. One year's labor over the fire, generally proved fatal yet as fast as one devotee passed away, there were found many willing and anxious to fill his place.

The Rattlesnake Trading Post, pictured above, was based out of Bluewater, New Mexico, and promised visitors the remains of a "48-foot-long prehistoric monster" in the late 1940s. If visitors dared to view the remains, they would see what the owners hoped to appear to be the bones of a giant rattlesnake. In reality, the remains were made by the owners out of various cow vertebrae mixed in with some plaster.

The Kansas City Journal of July 10, 1881, put a different spin on the snake and identified the great serpent as Montezuma's successor, ruling over the pueblo not as a mindless monster but as an intelligent deity. The paper explained:

> During [Montezuma's] absence a great snake assumed the functions of governor and was deified equally with his illustrious predecessor. On one occasion he became angry at his subjects and left the pueblo, taking up his abode in a neighboring mountain. This distressed his people who turned out en masse and importuned him to return, which he finally consented to do upon condition that an infant should be sacrificed to him every day. To

this his subjects agreed, and peace reigned over afterward.

Contrary to peace reigning ever after, a letter, dated October 4, 1883, out of Las Vegas, alleged that the constant human sacrifices were what caused the depopulation of Pecos:

> The town was abandoned, some say, [sic] Commanches attacked it and so reduced it that it could no longer continue, but another tradition has it that a sacred serpent was kept in the council house where the fire was burning; and that it was fed every day a child, and that reduced the Pueblo finally to a point where the few remaining could not hold out alone.[4]

As opposed to the snake devouring the population of the pueblo, others asserted that the snake was taken with the survivors to a new home. Adolph Bandelier heard the sacred snake had been taken by the last surviving pueblo residents to Jemez Pueblo. Bandelier's source for the tale was the same man who had told him tales of the sacred flame in 1880: Mariano Ruíz. Years later, Mariano Ruíz's grandson also mentioned the serpent to the famous photographer Edward S. Curtis in 1924. In Curtis's *The North American Indians* (Volume 17), and contrary to the account of his grandfather, Ruiz's grandson held that the snake had not been taken elsewhere. It had died.

> The snake, he said, was kept in an underground room in the village, and at stated intervals a newborn infant was fed to it. The elder Ruiz was asked to assume the duty of custodian of the sacred fire, an annual office, which he declined because he had observed that the fire-keeper always died soon after being released from confinement in the subterranean chamber where the fire burned. (Whether the fire and the serpent were housed in the same cell the grandson did not know, but possibly such was the case and the refusal of Ruiz to accept the proffered position was really due to his horror at the idea of spending a year in proximity to the reptile. But there

appears to be no good reason why he should not have imparted this information to Bandelier, if such was the case.) Strolling about the environs of the village, Ruiz one day came upon his most intimate friend bowed in grief. To the Mexican's inquiry the Indian responded that his newborn child had been condemned to be fed to the snake, that already he had been forced to yield several children to the sacrifice, and had vainly hoped that this one would be spared. This was the first time Ruiz had heard that children were fed to the snake. He proposed that they hoodwink the priests, and acting on his advice the Indian poisoned a newborn kid [baby goat] with certain herbs, wrapped it up as if it were a baby, and threw it to the reptile. That night terrifying sounds issued from the den as the great snake writhed in its death agony, and in the morning it lay with the white of its belly exposed. The populace was utterly downcast, for this presaged the extinction of the tribe.

Yet another variation of the end of the snake was unearthed by Helen H. Roberts in her article "The Reason for the Departure of the Pecos Indians for Jemez Pueblo" appearing in issue #34 of *American Anthropologist* in 1932. Roberts had gathered the account during the summers of 1929 and 1930 as she collected songs in the Rio Grande pueblos. At San Ildefonso she met 70-year-old Ignacio Aguilar who told her the "real reason" that Pecos Pueblo had been abandoned. The story came from Ignacio's grandfather who knew of the "snake god" the Pecos peoples kept concealed in a kiva. According to him, the snake god gave all that they asked so long as the hunters supplied fresh meat to it. (Notably, no mention was made of human sacrifice in this instance.) "The snake was very hungry and required much meat. It was just after a war, and the kiva men were very busy, or perhaps for some other reason they did not feed the snake god," Aguilar told Roberts. He continued that the snake spoke to the men, asking for food, and when his pleas were ignored, he told the men, "Since you will give me no food, I cannot stay and help the people any longer. I must go away from here."

A group watches dancers perform traditional dances on the San Ildefonso Pueblo in New Mexico, c.1940. (National Archives 2013-1578)

And so, the snake-god slithered out of the kiva and left a "track like a small arroyo" in his wake. Aguilar's grandfather and a party of San Ildefonso Indians happened to be out hunting near Galisteo when they saw two Pecos Indians coming from the river. The two hunters asked Aguilar's grandfather and his companions if they had seen the giant snake on its way to the river. When they replied that they had not, the Pecos men replied, "It is well that you did not, for he might have bitten you. We have tracked him this far, but we cannot find him."

The two Pecos hunters traveled down the valley, tracking the snake's path down to Domingo, where they lost it. The trail led into the river and the snake was never seen again. After that, Aguilar's grandfather claimed, the magic left Pecos Pueblo and so did its residents.

Josiah Gregg, too, would seem to have heard an account of the serpent's departure.

The story of this wonderful serpent was so firmly believed in by many ignorant people, that on one occasion I heard an honest ranchero assert, that upon entering the village very early on a winter's morning, he saw the huge trail of the reptile in the snow, as large as that of a dragging ox.[5]

The Rio Grande River in New Mexico. Did the sacred serpent slip into its waters never to be seen again?

But how much truth did these tales contain? Early day historian and explorer Charles Lummis was skeptical of them. In his book *Mesa, Cañon and Pueblo,* Lummis offered a lengthy discourse on the history of rattlesnakes being kept at various pueblos in New Mexico, not just Pecos:

> But while all snakes are to be treated well, the Pueblo holds the rattlesnake actually sacred. It is, except the rare Pichu-cuate (a real asp), the only venomous reptile in the Southwest, and is the only snake dignified by a place among "The Trues." Ch'a-ra-ra-de is not really worshiped by the Pueblos; but they hold it one of the sacred animals which are useful to "The Trues," and credited with wonderful powers. Up to a generation ago it played in the marvelously complicated civilization of these people a much more important part than it does to-day. In days of old, every Pueblo town maintained a huge rattlesnake, which was kept in its own sacred room and fed with great solemnity once a year. My own pueblo of Isleta used to support a sacred rattler in a volcanic

cave of the Cerro del Aire; and there was great consternation when it escaped. Old men have told me that it was nearly as large around as my body, which may be discounted. But I myself saw a sacred snake that escaped from Acoma and was killed by an American teamster; and it was as large as the thickest part of my thigh.[6]

Lummis also spoke to the stories of Pecos Pueblo, which he did not believe:

There used to be gruesome stories of human sacrifices to these sacred rattlers—even that a baby was chosen by lot from the pueblo once a year to be fed to the snake. That of course was a foolish fable. The Pueblos never practised human sacrifice in any form, even in prehistoric times; and the very grandfather of all the rattlesnakes could no more swallow the smallest baby than he could fly.[7]

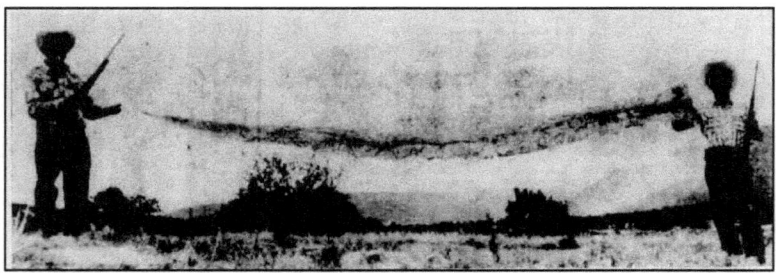

The image above, taken from the *Ruidoso News* of June 24, 1960, shows two cowboys holding up the skin of what they claimed to have been a giant rattlesnake that they shot in the lava fields near Carrizozo. The *Roswell Daily Record* of July 12, 1960, reported that one of the cowboys was "200 feet away when he opened fire, aiming at the monster's backbone. All eight bullets hit the snake, but none of them penetrated the telephone-pole thickness of the frightful thing...Baca said smoke appeared to come out of the snake's body when the bullets struck home, but said it was probably dust." The story was a sensation in New Mexico for a few days until it was finally determined that the 18-foot-long snakeskin came not from a giant rattlesnake, but from a dumpster in nearby Ruidoso. It was, in fact, an old python skin. The two pranksters acquired it and then concocted the tale of the giant rattlesnake.

Rather than dying, departing, or just not existing at all, a faithful few have speculated the serpent still lives. Like Montezuma, it awaits a grand return. New Mexico historian Alice Bullock wrote in *Living Legends of the Santa Fe Country* that

> ...there are those who say the holy serpent still sleeps today in a hidden cave somewhere close to the old ruin, awaiting the return of his worshippers. There are even stories that say the feathered serpent is lethargic because it has been so long since he has been fed a pueblo virgin, even though there seems to be nothing in pueblo lore to indicate they practiced human sacrifice.[8]

Chapter Notes

[1] Gregg, *Commerce of the Prairies*, p.189.

[2] Ibid.

[3] *Connersville Examiner*, October 10, 1883.

[4] Ibid.

[5] Gregg, *Commerce of the Prairies*, p.189.

[6] Lummis, *Mesa, Cañon and Pueblo*, pp.147-148.

[7] Ibid, p.148.

[8] Bullock, *Living Legends of Santa Fe*, p.52.

The Pinon Tree, pictured above in an old engraving from Arizona, is the state tree of New Mexico. As such, it is no surprise that Montezuma is associated with it as well.

7.

SACRED TREE OF PECOS
More Propaganda of the Mexican–American War?

Earlier was covered how the Mexican government manipulated the myth of Montezuma during the Mexican-American War. On the American side of the conflict was either their own piece of propaganda or an actual prophecy on the part of the Puebloans relating to the defeat of Mexico. The first inklings of this prophecy relating to the Mexican-American War first appeared in an article in the *Miami Helmet* of May 27, 1875. In it, the author claimed to have heard that Montezuma was not to return alone but with an army of men from the East, who would drive away the Spanish invaders. And indeed, the U.S. Army to some extent did fulfill this when they took Santa Fe in the Mexican-American War. The author of the article in the *Helmet* wrote, "After the arrival of Americans in Santa Fe, which was regarded as a part of the fulfillment of this promise, [the eternal] fire, in some manner, became extinguished…" Interestingly, this same article held that Pecos Pueblo was abandoned after the war, rather than before it in 1837 as is historically accurate.

There was another facet to the return of Montezuma in the Mexican-American War in the form of a sacred tree. The *Las Vegas Daily Gazette* of April 29, 1883, reported how at Pecos there "used to be a pinon tree which was planted by Montezuma." It was said that Montezuma and his priests used to sit in the shade of the tree while Montezuma prophesied and spoke in parables.

When Brigadier-General Stephen W. Kearny, pictured above, took Santa Fe in 1848, some regarded it as fulfilment of a prophecy given by Montezuma at Pecos Pueblo. (Engraving by T. B. Welch, *Graham's Magazine*, July 1849)

"Here he foretold, several centuries in advance of its occurrence, the Spanish invasion," the article claimed. Montezuma warned that the strange invaders would come from the south and make slaves of them for 250 years. However, their salvation rested upon the coming of "a white race of mighty warriors, gifted in the arts of war and peace, riding upon snow-white chargers," who would arrive from the east to rescue them. After this, the rains would return and the mountains would "yield up their treasures to the pale faces" and that "the people would grow rich and fat with herds of cattle and sheep." More specifically, this would occur upon the falling of the sacred tree planted by Montezuma.

The tradition of the sacred tree had been in existence for some time, as the *Oroville Weekly Butte Record* of October 9, 1858, also printed this prophecy, claiming that,

> Montezuma took a tall tree, and planted it in an inverted position, saying that when he should disappear a foreign race would rule over his people, and there would be no rain. But he commanded them to watch the sacred fire till that tree should fall at which time white men would pour into the land from the east, to overthrow their oppressors, and he himself would return to build up his kingdom. The earth would again be fertilized by rain, and the mountains yield treasures of silver or gold.

An article in the *El Paso Daily Herald* of November 12, 1900, reprinted a better account of the sacred tree, taken from Marion Hill, in Frank Leslie's *Popular Magazine*. According to the account, Montezuma's "brother gods" instructed him to "plant a tree upside down beside the chief estufa of Pecos." It continued that he should light a holy fire which was to be "kept burning until the tree fell, then would there come to the rescue of the oppressed a great pale face nation and deliver them from the Spanish thrall."

The piece concluded,

> So the fire was lit and a sentinel was posted to guard its sacred flame; and the tree was planted—under the circumstances the planter would be excusable in planting the tree as insecurely as possible. But year after year passed, and the tree remained standing Sentinel succeeded sentinel and the flame lived on. Generations withered away, yet deliverance seemed no nearer. One day there came a rumor from old Santa Fe that the city had surrendered to a white-faced people. Was this the band of deliverers? That day at noon the sacred tree toppled and fell. Spanish rule was no more. The prophecy had been fulfilled.

The *Las Vegas Daily Gazette* of April 29, 1883, made the same case that the prophecy had been fulfilled by General Stephen W. Kearny as well:

This prediction, made before or after the fact, as the case may be, was strangely fulfilled in 1847, for the day after the tree fell by the force of a mighty wind, the gallant Kearny came down the valley, mounted upon a magnificent white stallion, at the head of 3,000 pale-faced soldiers, and tipped over the deputy throne that the Viceroy Armijo had set up at Santa Fe.

The pious Pueblos believe that Kearney was their deliverer from the Spanish yoke, and every morning when they go to the house to look for the coming of Montezuma, they take from the buckskin pouches they wear upon their breast, a pinch of sacred powder made from the flour of parched corn, and puff it into the air, breathing a prayer for the repose of Kearny's soul,[1] and begging a blessing from Montezuma, and the sun which he taught them to worship, upon the work of the day.

The *Inter Ocean* of August 22, 1897, said more or less the same thing but concluded, "Strangely enough the fall of the tree was coincident with the entry of General Kearny into Santa Fe, but the remainder of the prophecy is yet unfulfilled." Ultimately, the story of the tree is lesser-known when compared to that of the eternal flame and the sacred serpent. And most importantly, as the *Inter Ocean* article concluded, the prophecy is indeed unfulfilled.

Chapter Notes

[1] Kearny died not long after the war ended, on October 31, 1848.

8.

TREASURE OF PECOS
Great Montezuma's Ghost!

Although most Pecos-based tales of Montezuma had him depart Pecos for Mexico, there was at least one story to the contrary that Montezuma died at Pecos. In the case of that story, he became a treasure guardian, or what the Spanish called the *patrón*. This particular tale was unearthed by famous folklorist J. Frank Dobie, who heard it from an individual named José Vaca, a resident of Pecos in the early 20th century.[1] According to Vaca in *Coronado's Children*, the *patrón* was "the dead man who guards the treasure. All these peoples long time ago who hide great treasure been careful to have *patrón*."[2]

Vaca told Dobie of a Pecos Indian who had been jailed in Las Vegas on a rape charge. As the Pecos Indians' execution method for a rape crime was to strip the accused naked and tie them down over an ant den to be picked clean, the sheriff agreed to let the prisoner get away in the night. Out of gratitude, the prisoner told the sheriff of Montezuma's lost gold buried under Pecos Church.

In this variation, Montezuma was a half-Spanish half-Pueblo Indian chief who loved the Indian side of his lineage more so than the Spanish. And, somehow this Montezuma still possessed a great horde of gold like his Aztec namesake. This gold he wished to remain hidden until the Spanish had been driven from the land, similar to the legend of the sacred tree covered earlier. According to the prisoner, the treasure was the "great secret of all the Indians of the Pecos Country."[3]

Old postcard depicting the ruins at Pecos.

The story went that as Montezuma was dying, he instructed his people to dig a big hole next to his pueblo and place his gold down in it. Next, the weakened old chief ordered his people to place him in the hole, so that his ghost could guard the treasure. Or, in other words, Montezuma was buried alive with the gold to await death. His last command was that the gold was not to be unearthed until the Spanish had vacated the Indian's land.

The prisoner told the sheriff that if he journeyed to the church at Pecos, off to the side of the road, he should find a distinct white rock. Within the rock, he would find a small wooden cross wedged into one of the cracks. This signified the spot of the treasure, which was next to a black rock sitting over a cave. The instructions were to dig beneath the white rock, under which he would find the grave of Montezuma himself. Then, seven feet beneath Montezuma would be the treasure horde. However, the treasure was watched over not only by the great chief's ghost, but by secretive pueblo men as well. If the sheriff were to dig up the gold, he had best go at night with a car ready to speed away with the gold at once.

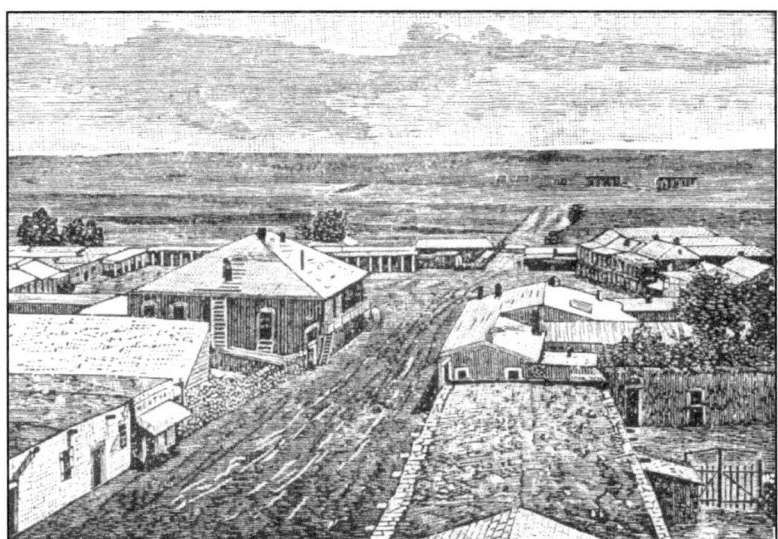

West Las Vegas 1880 taken from H.T. Wilson's *Historical Sketch of Las Vegas*, published 1880.

The sheriff rounded up a friend, none other than the teller of the tale, José Vaca. The duo was ready to go dig for the gold, but the sheriff's wife was too afraid of the treasure curse and begged her husband not to go. Vaca himself searched for the white rock on his own but could never find it, blaming Montezuma's ghost. "I cannot understand this *patrón*," he told Dobie. "I am strong man. [Montezuma] is dead, but he keep me off. I wish I know when he sleep."[4]

Dobie also collected a tale concerning bewitched sand at Pecos Pueblo from José Vaca. José told how many years ago, his grandfather had bought a piece of land at Pecos from a Pecos Indian. "You have here now more wealth than is in the world elsewhere," he told the man.[5]

When the man asked what he meant, the Indian took him to the land and began collecting what appeared to be ordinary sand from the creek. They loaded it onto a mule and took it to sell. Inside was $25 worth of gold in the sand. After the Indian had moved away as planned, José's grandfather returned to the spot and collected several more bags of sand, loading them onto two burros. However, this time when he went to sell, he found no gold in the sand whatsoever.

José told Dobie that maybe the Indian "was un brujo [a wizard]. Maybe the sand was *embrujada* [bewitched]."[6] José surmised, "I know when the Indian is here the sand has gold. I know when the Indian is gone the gold is all gone too."[7]

Vaca never did find the treasure, but did find a large white rock that used to have a wooden cross embedded in it, so perhaps the story of Montezuma's grave from earlier had become conflated with this alleged treasure cave.

Chapter Notes

[1] Presumably, Dobie collected it in the 1920s or thereabouts, as the book it appears in, *Coronado's Children*, was first published in 1930.
[2] Dobie, *Coronado's Children*, p.205.
[3] Ibid.
[4] Ibid, p.206.
[5] Ibid, p.198.
[6] Ibid, p.199.
[7] Ibid.

9.

STONE FOOTPRINTS AT PECOS
More Legends of Montezuma

One of the more interesting legends of ancient peoples is that of the footprints of a god-like figure in the rock. Adrienne Mayor devoted a whole book, *Fossil Legends of the First Americans*, to the stories told by indigenous peoples to explain fossils of large, prehistoric animals along with legends revolving around preserved footprints, which indigenous peoples often attributed to gods and demigods that may have walked the land. All the way up near Jamestown, New York, the Onondagas had a set of hand and footprints that they venerated as those of the Great Spirit when he once visited earth, for instance.

In the Southwest, the two most popular figures to leave their footprints in stone were probably Montezuma and Quetzalcoatl. W.E. Curtis said of Pecos that "The old town of Pecos was no doubt a fortified pueblo of the Aztecs, and stands today, as it has stood for many centuries, built upon a great rock, which bears the shape of a human foot."[1]

Along the same lines, the *Connersville Examiner* of October 10, 1883, printed a letter out of Las Vegas that stated, "Near by [the church] are some boulders having in them distinct imprints of human feet, as plain as if they were in soft clay, and the tradition is that these are prints of Montezuma's feet when he left."[2]

An excellent example of fossilized footprints in New Mexico are those at White Sands, photographed above, along with their discoverer, Ellis Wright, c.1932. Initially, they were thought to have been the footsteps of a giant, but later finds revealed they were actually made by a prehistoric giant ground sloth rather than a giant human. (Above courtesy Wright's niece, Terri Bunt)

The *Las Vegas Gazette* of November 18, 1876, reported on the mysterious prints in their article "Footprints on the Sands of Time." In full, it read:

In New Mexico many ancient ruins of an ancient race of inhabitants are found, and also veritable foot prints in the solid rock. If the traveler en route to Santa Fe from this city, will take the trouble he can verify the fact. On the stage road near the ruins of the old Pecos Pueblo, a ledge of sand rock juts out across the road. On the left hand side, an examination of the surface of the rocks, will reveal human footprints in the solid rock. The impressions are perfect. Some are large, evidently those of grown persons, others are small, the tracks of children. Some were made by the naked foot, others by feet encased in moccasins. There is no mistake or fraud in the matter, footprints are there in the solid rock.

Who made them and how were they made? We did not have the time or take the trouble to determine the geological period to which this particular stratum of rock belongs. Undoubtedly it was fashioned at the bottom of the sea, a few million years before Adam's time. We do not think the foot prints were made at the time the rocks were formed, but we do think they were made a few hundred, or perhaps a thousand years ago. The rocks evidently formed, at one time, the bed of a small creek flowing nearby. At that time the footprints were made. The water softened the surface of the rock sufficiently to take the impression from the feet of the Indians playing in the water; or else the tracks were made in a layer of sand and mud. The creek in time cut a new and deeper channel leaving these rocks high and dry. They again became baked and hardened, retaining the footprint. The action of the elements has not been able to erase them. A track in sand rock would be more lasting than in many other kinds. Sand is but slightly soluble and if the surface was sufficiently hard to prevent washing away, it would not be dissolved.

Chapter Notes

[1] Curtis, "The Pecos Legend," *Las Vegas Daily Gazette* (April 29, 1883).
[2] Mexico has similar legends at spots where Quetzalcoatl left his footprints, and so on.

PART III

Montezuma in Arizona

MONTEZUMA CASTLE, ARIZONA.
June 5, 1929. GHE.

10.

MONTEZUMA & THE PAPAGO
Montezuma in Creation Myths

In great contrast to the Pueblo peoples of New Mexico, who viewed Montezuma as a Christ-type figure, the indigenous peoples of Arizona and northern Mexico made Montezuma out to be more of a god-man with a penchant for Old Testament wrath. In the *Journal of American Folklore*, the famous anthropologist J. Alden Mason recorded that the Papago feared Montezuma "because of his powerful magic, with which he could work them much harm."[1]

Mason heard tales of Montezuma from Abraham Pablo at the then-newly established Papago Reservation in Santa Rosa, Arizona, in 1919. As Mason noted, this was a wider myth tailored to Santa Rosa, as most of it took place there. Like many others of the time, Mason was perplexed by the inclusion of Montezuma in the story. On the first page of his discourse, he noted the curious association between Montezuma and the creator god of the O'odham peoples of Arizona, called I'itoi, or Elder Brother:

> One of the interesting features of the present myth is the identification of Elder Brother with Montezuma. The reason for this is not clear; but that the identification is a uniform one, is indicated by the number of localities in the Papago country which bear the name of Montezuma.[2]

Pablo's version of the story began similarly to the Biblical account of the Tower of Babel, wherein all the people spoke a common language. Not only that, back then, people could even speak and be spoken to by the animals. Elder Brother was good to the people, causing the rain to fall and water their crops. In charge of all the people at the time was the benevolent Chief Montezuma.

J. Alden Mason at the ruins of Uxmal in Mexico in 1932.

For reasons unknown, one day Montezuma turned on his people and supernaturally began inflicting pain upon them. And so the people stormed his abode and killed him. However, four days later, Montezuma was discovered alive and well.[3] And so the people returned to kill him again. To make sure he stayed dead, they cut up his body and crushed his bones to dust, burying all his remains in the earth. Again, four days later, Montezuma was whole again. The people attacked him for a third time. After he was dead, they cooked his flesh until it melted off the bone and poured him into the earth.

Yet again, Montezuma returned, and so all the people came together to discuss a way to kill him. One suggested they beseech Yellow Buzzard to slay him with his iron bow. Yellow Buzzard agreed and shot Montezuma with an arrow. Four days later, Montezuma still lay dead on his doorstep. Finally, it appeared that the great ruler would not resurrect.

This time, it took Montezuma four years to revive, and when he did, he was angrier than ever. Montezuma's spirit ascended to the sun to plot his revenge. There he remained for another four years, constructing a new man from the ashes of burned feathers among other things. This man he sent to the earth to deceive his people. The man of Montezuma appeared at the local watering hole and enticed a man from the village to ingest a strange liquid. When he did so, the man began to sprout feathers and turned into a giant eagle. Montezuma's emissary returned to the sun, leaving the giant eagle alone.

A Papago Man photographed by George P. Thresher, 1900.

People from the village spotted the giant bird and began trying to shoot it from the sky, not knowing it was a member of their tribe, so the eagle fled to a great mesa where it nested. Around the same time, Montezuma's old bones began to stir with life, and his spirit returned to them. Again, Montezuma walked among the people, but this time they were too afraid to confront him. Mason explained, "So he lived among his people again... [but] they were much afraid of him, and did not like to have him go among the houses."[4]

Papago Indians at the well.
Southern Arizona.

The great eagle Montezuma had created was also on a killing spree, devouring so much game that there was nothing left for the people to hunt. When the eagle had killed nearly all the game, it turned its eye to the villagers. Montezuma took note of this, and decided that he would slay the bird of prey, but only after it had taken one of the villagers. Soon the great eagle carried a man to its nest and killed him. The terrified villagers pondered how they might defeat the eagle lest it devour them all.

The people became so desperate, they sought out their old chief for help, just as he had planned. However, Montezuma told them he would kill the eagle only after four years had passed. It was a terrible time for the villagers, as the winged monster carried off one to two men per day. One day, the eagle abducted a young woman, but did not eat her. Instead, he made her his wife and she bore him a son.

At the end of the four years, Montezuma set out to slay the eagle as promised. He scaled the mesa while the eagle was away and conferred with his wife, who told him of her husband's habits and also agreed to aid in his killing. Knowing when the eagle would return, Montezuma transformed himself into a fly and hid within a pile of dead bodies in the cave. He also warned the woman to find a firm place to hide, because when he killed the eagle, the mesa was liable to shake itself apart.

Late in the night, Montezuma resumed human form, and crept up on the eagle. With a machete, he cut off the head of the eagle and also that of its offspring. He then chopped the bodies up into pieces and cast them off in the four corners of the wind as the mesa shook. Then, Montezuma went to the pile of corpses, which the eagle chose for some reason not to eat, and sprinkled water on them.[5] The dead returned to life, and with Montezuma, all climbed down the mesa and returned to the village.

Montezuma did not receive the hero's welcome he anticipated, and still the people feared him. And so, through contrived means, Montezuma constructed yet another monster to terrify the people. To do so, he created yet another new man, who, by trickery, caused a woman to become pregnant. Mason explained,

> When the baby was born, it had long finger-nails like a bear, and the parents wanted to kill it, but the mother refused. This monster was known as *ho'o'kE*...[6]

As the monstrous baby grew into a monstrous woman, it became a she-demon along the lines of Lillith and La Llorona, preying upon infants. Specifically, she took them back to her cave and ground up their entrails for food. The people again beseeched Montezuma for help. Now living in a cave, an emissary approached and asked Montezuma if he would kill the *ho'o'kE* as he did the great eagle. He agreed, and this time waited only four days rather than four years to exterminate the creature.

Montezuma staged a party at the village and enticed the *ho'o'kE* to dance with him. This she did to her great delight, and after four straight days, finally became exhausted and passed out. Montezuma slung her over his shoulders and took her back to his cave, where the villagers had built a fire pyre. Montezuma tossed her on the pyre and lit it. When the *ho'o'kE* awoke, she jumped so high she hit the ceiling of the cave, causing it to split. Montezuma then put his foot down on the crack, causing it to close again and also creating a footprint that locals claimed could still be seen.[7]

The *ho'o'kE* perished in the flames, and the people happily carried away her remains. But Montezuma had still not regained their trust, and so he set out to consult with chiefs in other lands. The chiefs of the North, South, West, and East all told him that they could not think of a way to help him, though the latter suggested Montezuma seek out the aid of the chief in the underworld. And so there Montezuma went. There, the chief of the underworld told him that perhaps his people would trust and revere him, so why not kill all the inhabitants of the surface and let the people of the underworld take their place?

Depiction of the Aztec version of the emergence myth.

And so, Montezuma led the peoples of the underworld to the surface, and with the aid of a medicine woman, set out killing all those on the earth. After a long saga of battling shamans too lengthy to be recounted here, the people of the underworld had truly taken over the surface. (However, just to keep them on their toes, Montezuma set the Apache apart to serve as enemies to the other tribes.)

The story ended rather abruptly, with two men from Heaven coming to try and get Montezuma to go to a council far away. When Montezuma refused to go, they sealed him in an underground home with four doorways somewhere around what is today the Arizona/Mexico state line. "And there is Montezuma locked up," the tale concluded.[8]

Overall, this myth presented an interesting juxtaposition of Biblical and Native American creation stories. In particular, it presented a unique variation of the ideas of past worlds. In many cases, when tribes emerged to the surface, the idea was that they were leaving behind a past world and entering a new one as opposed to simply emerging from beneath the surface of the earth. That the residents of the previous world killed those of the new one is different from many others that this author has seen, though.

Chapter Notes

[1] Mason, "The Papago Migration Legend," *Journal of American Folklore* (Vol. 34, No. 133, Jul. - Sep., 1921), p.259.
[2] Ibid, p.254.
[3] The number four is likely significant, as it is revered by many tribes in conjunction with the four cardinal directions.
[4] Mason, "The Papago Migration Legend," *Journal of American Folklore* (Vol. 34, No. 133, Jul. - Sep., 1921), p.259.
[5] This bears some similarities to stories of Quetzalcoatl sprinkling his blood on the dead in the underworld and returning them to life.
[6] Mason, "The Papago Migration Legend," *Journal of American Folklore* (Vol. 34, No. 133, Jul. - Sep., 1921), p.262.
[7] Presumably, this was a way of explaining a real stone footprint somewhere in the area.
[8] Mason, "The Papago Migration Legend," *Journal of American Folklore* (Vol. 34, No. 133, Jul. - Sep., 1921), p.267.

11.

MONTEZUMA & THE FLOOD

The Adventures of Montezuma and Coyote

Again demonstrating how the Arizona iteration of Montezuma differed from the New Mexico version was this myth. Essentially, it was a telling Genesis, complete with creation, the flood, and the Tower of Babel, but starring Montezuma and Coyote. Hubert Howe Bancroft corralled this particular Montezuma legend from Chief Con Quien of the Tohono O'odham. It was published in the Indian Affairs Report of 1865 and went that, in the beginning, the Great Spirit was digging a hole when he found clay for the first time. He molded the clay into a man and dropped it into the Earth. The clay man turned into Montezuma, making him the Adam of this creation legend in a way.

Actually, Montezuma led from out of the earth a race of preexisting people, who then populated the surface. Montezuma next taught the people all there was to know, from basket-making to planting corn. Notably, at that time, the sun was closer to the earth. As such, there was no winter yet. All the people and the animals spoke a common language until a Great flood devastated the world. Montezuma and Coyote, the trickster, survived because Coyote warned of the oncoming cataclysm. Montezuma created a canoe for himself, which he had parked atop Santa Rosa Mountain. Coyote had also fashioned a boat, gnawing down a giant cane and filling the holes with gum.

AN INDIAN TRADITION.

The Story of the Deluge on This Continent.

From the Detroit Post.

The following rather singular tradition which exists among the Papago Indians, respecting Montezuma, their founder, and the deluge, has, we believe, never yet appeared in print; at least not in its present shape. It was related by Captain Con Quan, an aged and intelligent member of the tribe, and was taken down from his lips by an interpreter for Judge Henry T. Backus, of Arizona Territory, and formerly of this city. Judge Backus has visited many of the places mentioned in the legend, and has been an eyewitness of the quadrennial feast still celebrated at the cave. He represents the Papagoes as being nominally Catholics, yet clinging to their national traditions with great tenacity, and cherishing the memory of Montezuma with even more than saintly veneration.

The tradition of the deluge is interesting in its relation to the origin of the Indians of the country, and especially the ancient tribes who lived in the twilight of civilization, until the Spanish Christians annihilated them. Did they bring this tradition with them from the Asiatic Continent? Or, did they come in contact with the people of the Old World, antecedent to any historical evidence of that fact, from whom they derived this tradition?

These are inquiries naturally suggested by the following narrative. Montezuma, it will be understood, is not the monarch of that name whom Cortes dethroned. It is the generic term of their rulers, like Pharaoh, Cæsar, &c.

This issue of the *Philadelphia Inquirer* of November 17, 1869, reprinted another Montezuma flood legend. (See Appendix I for the full article)

The duo boarded their respective boats, and later met atop Monte Rosa after the waters subsided. In the aftermath of the deluge, the Great Spirit repopulated the Earth, and Montezuma was left in charge of humanity once more. However, as in the previous myth, for some reason, Montezuma became proud and wicked. Montezuma felt there was no longer a need for a creator god and that he should assume the role. Despite often being portrayed as a devilish trickster, it was Coyote who warned Montezuma against such a foolish act in this story.

Illustration from *Indian Days of the Long Ago*, c.1915.

Montezuma then broke off his friendship with Coyote and rebelled against the Great Spirit by commanding humanity to build a house that reached the heavens so that he may kill the Great Spirit.[1] Initially, the Great Spirit came to earth to try and reason with Montezuma, but the evil king would have none of it. This, they said, was why men became evil and took to hunting animals for food. Men also turned against one another for the first time, making war. As a warning, the Great Spirit moved the sun away from the earth, bringing about the first winter. Mankind did not heed the omen though, and continued construction of the great house that would ascend to heaven.

The great house, it was said, had rooms of coral and jet, turquoise and mother-of-pearl. Once the great house broke through the clouds, the Great Spirit struck down the jeweled tower with thunderbolts. He also caused the language of the people to become confused. Nor could humankind communicate with the animals anymore as they used to.

The Tower of Babel by Pieter Bruegel the Elder c.1563.

Montezuma was still not humbled and shook his fist at the sky and again renounced the Great Spirit. Angry, Montezuma commanded that all temples to the Great Spirit be destroyed. As punishment, the Great Spirit sent a locust to the east to summon a group of war-like invaders. Not long after, the Spanish conquistadors came ashore in Central America, and the evil Montezuma was vanquished once and for all, thus tying the mythical Montezuma in with the historical one.

Chapter Notes

---

[1] Though often overlooked in modern translations of the Bible, there was an implication that Nimrod was trying to ascend to Heaven and kill God, which is present in this story with Montezuma and the Great Spirit.

THE SACRED SERPENT IN ARIZONA

The 1870s and 1880s were tumultuous decades for the Apache in Arizona. In 1881, Geronimo famously led the White Mountain Apaches in a breakout from the reservation. Preceding this was a semi-famous skirmish between the soldiers of Fort Apache and some Coyotero Apache at Cibecue Creek on August 30, 1881. Even some Apache scouts with the soldiers mutinied to join their Coyotero brethren in the fight. As stated before, the historical ramifications of the conflict had the White Mountain Apache leaving the reservation to join forces with Geronimo and head to Mexico.

A medicine man of note named Nock-ay-det-klinne was the driving force behind the incident at Cibecue Creek. Stories circulated about the shaman that made him sound more like a medieval sorcerer. For instance, Nock-ay-det-klinne claimed that to help the Apache in their struggle against the White Eyes that he would raise the slain Apache chief Diablo from the dead. And, indeed, Chief Nana claimed that during a Ghost Dance Nock-ay-det-klinne conjured the spirits of Mangas Coloradas, Cochise, and Victorio from the ground. Stories even circulated that because the white man lusted so badly for gold, Nock-ay-det-klinne had forged golden bullets with which to kill the soldiers.

Cut from the same cloth as tales of Nock-ay-det-klinne raising spirits from the dead is a story related in Brad and Sherry Steiger's book, *Montezuma's Serpent and Other True Supernatural Tales of the Southwest*. According to the Steigers, in the 1870s there was a cruel Indian trader by the name of Malcolm Graves living in the White Mountains region.[1] It was said that Graves made slaves of the Apache indebted to him and took the women as mistresses against their will. Others he tortured simply for the sake of cruelty and perverse amusement.

An Apache medicine man identified as Patch in the story went on a ten-day fast to beseech the spirit of Montezuma to come and help him. Patch succeeded in summoning Montezuma's spirit, and the great ruler agreed to help him. To this end, he sent his gigantic rattlesnake to come and devour the evil Graves and his wife, Antonia. The serpent did so, the Apache slaves were freed, and the spirits of Malcolm and Antonia were sent to the netherworld for purification. However, considering the ghosts of the duo can still be seen at the site of the trading post by campers, it would seem they were never purified.

Specifically, the Steigers claimed that at the turn of the century, a hunter and his wife encountered several ghostly figures in the ruins of the trading post. Ghostly screams of the dead Apache slaves were heard, and a hulking man-like figure was seen in the woods. In the doorway of the ruined post was seen the silhouette of a woman, possibly Antonia. Lastly, the one-eyed medicine man, Patch, appeared to the couple. By his side was Montezuma's giant rattlesnake, reared up as tall as the medicine man himself. The ghostly medicine man beseeched the couple to flee, and so they did. Unfortunately, the Steigers did not cite any sources for the story, so its origins are a bit nebulous.

Section Notes

---

[1] The Steigers mentioned the last name of Reeves as an alternative.

12.

The Castle and the Well

Even more so than in New Mexico, Montezuma left his mark on the maps of Arizona. That state has five landmarks bearing Montezuma's name, the most famous of which is easily Montezuma Castle and the nearby Montezuma Well. Located in the Verde River Valley of Central Arizona, Montezuma Castle is famous as one of the most recognizable cliff palaces in the Southwest. It's also infamous for its namesake having nothing to do with it.

Largely due to any ancient ruin being associated with Montezuma, early settlers thought that the ruins were built by Aztec refuges who had fled northward to escape the Spanish invaders and decided to call the impressive cliff dwellings Montezuma Castle.[1] The name stuck, and because the beautiful oasis nearby was so close, it was called Montezuma's Well.

Rather than Aztec refugees, anthropologists think that the occupants of Montezuma Castle were peaceful farmers called the Sinagua and lived there from the 1100s into the 1400s.[2] The cliff dwellings are located about halfway up a 145-foot-high cliff face within a naturally made shallow depression. The five-story ruin has twenty rooms in its complex and, though not as grand as the cliff dwellings at Mesa Verde, still lives up to its name.[3]

Thomas Penfield related an interesting piece of lore on the castle in his book, *Dig Here!*, writing that, "A cowboy once swapped a horse for the castle, then traded the castle for two horses."[4]

Montezuma Castle was designated as a national monument by President Theodore Roosevelt in 1908. In his book, *Haunted Arizona*, author Charles Stansfield Jr. noted how initially visitors were allowed to go inside the complex's rooms up until 1951. Park officials put a stop to it after they determined the constant flow of visitors was deteriorating the interior of the castle. "There are those, however, who believe that the ghosts of Montezuma Castle were being disturbed, and becoming more agitated, by the hordes of visitors," Stansfield wrote.[5]

Stansfield recorded that before the rooms were closed to the general public, stories circulated of phantom Sinagua amidst the ruins. A notable encounter had a teenage Sinagua girl seen weaving a basket which would disappear in a swirl of dust. Another ghostly view, that of two women roasting meat over a fire, was accompanied by the phantom smell of cooked meat. Other ghostly scenes weren't so peaceful, with a phantom warrior sneaking into the room of a ghostly sleeper only to bash him over the head with a club. In another room could be seen a beheaded corpse, the severed head of which would come to life, its eyes popping open and a soundless scream coming from its mouth. In a little plaza on the fourth level, two warriors were said to be seen wrestling in eternal combat.

Stansfield noted that while Park Rangers officially denied these ghost stories, others have anonymously submitted ghostly sightings of their own.

MONTEZUMA WELL, NEAR PRESCOTT, ARIZONA.

The historical marker positioned before Montezuma Well, pictured above, notes that "Traditional stories of the Yavapai and Apache people say that once something emerges from the vents at the bottom of the Well, it can never return."

Not too far from Montezuma Castle is Montezuma Well, which sports a few cliff-dwelling ruins of its own. Technically, the well is really a limestone sink about 470 feet in diameter and 55 feet deep. It is kept full of water at a rate of 1,000 gallons a minute via subterranean thermal springs. The Sinagua tribe diverted the well's water, which should have flown into Beaver Creek, to use for irrigation.

Naturally, the well sported its share of fantastic legends. One attested that Cortés possessed a deerskin map bearing "Montezuma Well" as a place name on it. Another went that the Aztec treasure procession traveled to Montezuma Well and tossed the treasure into the depths rather than let the Spaniards get their hands on it. From this spot it was also thought that the plumed serpent of the Hopi had emerged. More than just a water source, the Sinagua believed the well was the entrance to the underworld. However, rather than Hades, the underworld in this instance referred more so to the previous world, out of which people climbed to reach the new world. The people lived in that world for many years and prospered until the chief took "an earthly bride, a sin for which the penalty was death."[6] As consequence, the Great Spirit sent a massive deluge to flood the underworld until it overflowed, forcing them to the next world.

Postcard of Montezuma Well.

Chapter Notes

[1] Schroeder & Hastings, *Montezuma Castle*, p.2.
[2] The name Sinagua meant people without water. The Sinagua, much like the Anasazi, disappeared from Montezuma Wells in 1500 A.D. Their final fate is a mystery, though some think they conjoined with the Hopi.
[3] On the note of Colorado's Mesa Verde, it is located in Montezuma County, by the way.
[4] Penfield, *Dig Here!*, p.61. However, Penfield was likely mixing up Montezuma Castle with Montezuma Well. The National Parks Service relates a local legend of an area rancher by the name of Abraham Smith purchasing the land around the well in 1887 for one horse, then selling the land back in 1889 for a team of horses.
[5] Stansfield, *Haunted Arizona*, p91.
[6] *Arizona Daily Sun* (June 24, 1976).

13.

MUMMIES OF MONTEZUMA CASTLE
Little People of the Southwest

Every culture has its legend of the little people, from the ancient Leprechauns of Ireland to the more recent gremlins of the early 20th century. These little people, similar to but not to be confused with fairies, were always magical but mischievous. Lewis and Clark heard tales of devilish little people in South Dakota during their famous expedition. Many years later, the body of one may have been found in the San Pedro Mountains of Wyoming in 1932. The Apache also had their mystical little people. An honest account of one was reprinted in Sherry Robinson's book *Apache Voices*. Specifically, the witness was Eugene Chihuahua, who told Eve Ball that as a child he had observed one of the little people high on a mountaintop.

> I thought at first that he was another child about two or three years old and that he might be lost from his mother but when I got close I saw that he was a grown man, not a child. There are little people living in the forest and they sometimes come around the outskirts of a rancheria [village] but never inside. They are not ghosts nor witches but just small people who never die. And they mean good to the Apaches.[1]

FIND PREHISTORIC
MUMMY IN CLIFFS

A prehistoric mummy only 32 inches long, with 20 teeth instead of the usual 28, with three fingers on each hand and four toes on the left foot, —the right foot is missing entirely— was recently discover by Jack Wilson and Mrs. Dovey Smith in a cliff dwelling near Wilson's place, which is six miles above the Windmill ranch on the east side of the Verde.

Though a hundred or more mummified dwarfs have been found in the cliff dwellings along the Verde and Beaver creek, this is the first that has not had a full complement of fingers, toes and teeth. It is believed that he was a freak.

The mummy discovered by Wilson and Mrs. Smith was wrapped in coarse cotton cloth and had cotton which still contained seeds. It was determined long ago by scientists that the prehistoric races which inhabited this region grew cotton and wove cloth.

The *Phoenix Arizona Republican* (May 1, 1922).

The United Verde Mine as depicted on an old postcard.

As it turns out, while Chihuahua may have been wrong about the little people never dying, evidence was found in Arizona near Montezuma Castle proving that Little People may have existed in the Southwest, just like the San Pedro Mountains mummy. *The Phoenix Arizona Republican* published a story on the find on May 1, 1922:

> A prehistoric mummy only 32 inches long; with 20 teeth instead of the usual 28, with three fingers on each hand and four toes on the left foot—the right foot is missing entirely—was recently discovered by Jack Wilson and Mrs. Dovey Smith in a cliff dwelling near Wilson's place, which is six miles above the Windmill ranch on the east side of the Verde.
>
> Though a hundred or more mummified dwarfs have been found in the cliff dwellings along the Verde and Beaver creek, this is the first that has not had a full complement of fingers, toes and teeth. It is believed that he was a freak.
>
> The mummy discovered by Wilson and Mrs. Smith was wrapped in coarse cotton cloth and had cotton which still contained seeds. It was determined long ago by scientists that the prehistoric races which inhabited this region grew cotton and wove cloth.

105

The San Pedro Mountains Mummy, which is similar to the Little People of New Mexico and Arizona.

The right foot had been broken off and it has not yet been located. A number of other human bones are in the same cave and the missing foot may be among them.

Those who have examined the mummy, which is now at Wilson's farm, declare that the teeth are well formed and evidently those of an adult, thus disposing of the theory that the mummy may be the remains of an infant. The head is well formed and it

UNUSUAL MUMMY FOUND

Race of Dwarfs Believed to Have Once Inhabited Part of This Country.

An unusual mummy, only thirty-two inches long and believed to have belonged to a race of dwarfs, has been discovered in a cliff dwelling near Wilson's ranch on the east side of the Verde, according to a report received at Los Angeles, Cal., from Jerome, Ariz.

The pygmy has only twenty teeth, three fingers and a thumb on one hand, and four toes on the left foot. The right foot is missing.

The shortage of teeth, fingers and toes appear to have been natural with the individual, though hardly a racial trait, because at least one hundred mummies have been found in the cliff and cave dwellers along the Verde and on Beaver Creek, and this is the first one found not naturally constituted. The teeth and head are perfectly formed and undoubtedly belonged to an adult and not a child.

is believed that the owner was not a person of defective mentality, regardless of his stature and shortage of digits.

Years ago a government archaeologist found over 30 tiny mummies in a cliff dwelling near Montezuma's castle. All of those had normally formed hands and feet but information as to the number of their teeth is lacking. In height they ranged from 18 to 36 inches. These mummies are now in the Smithsonian institution at Washington. D.C. Some others were disinterred near the mouth of Oak creek but their bones were simply thrown upon the ground and are still to be found there.

For a long time the theory that the aborigines of this section mummified their dead children was generally held but many competent investigators finally reached the conclusion that at one time there were a race of dwarfs in the Verde country.

Every cave in which the mummies have been found bears evidence of having been fired and many believe that the dwarfs were exterminated by the ancestors of the Indians that were here when the white man came.

MUMMY OF A CHILD.

A different article specified that the discoverer of the mummies twenty years ago was John Love. While I could find no mentions of Love finding the mummies, I did find many mentions of him in Flagstaff from the time at least.[2] The find from twenty years ago may have been one that occurred in 1896, which was published in the *Flagstaff Coconino Weekly Sun* of March 19, 1896, on the front page:

A PREHISTORIC MUMMY.
Prospectors Make Some Interesting Discoveries
Monday a party of prospectors on their way from Phoenix to Mangus, Colorado, stopped in town for a few hours. On their way here they spent a week at Montezuma Wells and at Montezuma's Castle, on Beaver creek. At the later place there are a large number of prehistoric cliff dwellings, which the party investigated. They found the former burying ground of the extinct race and unearthed twenty skeletons. They were fortunate enough to find one mummified body, the first one, it is believed, that has been found, and they propose to lake the mummy to Denver, where they expect to sell it.

Dr. D.J. Branneu was given an opportunity to examine the mummy and describes it as being a fine specimen and well preserved. The mummy is that of an adult male and of a pigmy race. It measured three and one half feet in length. Of the skeletons found by the party none of them exceeded that height, which seems to have been the greatest stature obtained by the unknown race of people that once inhabited all this portion of Arizona.

It is unfortunate that the mummy could not be purchased from the travelers, as it should be in the possession of some one of our historical societies, and should remain in territory instead of some Eastern museum.

The Jerome News gives an extended account of the alleged finding of a mummy in the United Verde mine. The finding of a mummy is a possible thing, but this alleged discovery coming on the heels of the finding of the bogus petrified man will make the story to be received with a large decoction of salt. After giving a very plausible account of the discovery the News spoils the story by claiming it to be that of Montezuma, the Aztec chief.

This blurb in the *Bisbee Cochise Review* of December 22, 1900, claimed that the mummy of Montezuma himself had been found in United Verde mine. See page 111 for more.

For many years, it was wondered if tales of the mummies of Montezuma Castle were true or not. About 43 years after the 1896 article, Earl Jackson, the custodian of Montezuma Castle at the time, found proof of the story. Evidence came in the form of photographs mailed to Jackson by S.L. Palmer Jr of San Francisco, California. The photographs showed Palmer's father along with Richard Wetherill, a well-known Navajo trading post owner, excavating ruins in Montezuma Castle

The *Arizona Daily Star* of August 4, 1939, reported,

> Following a guided trip through the prehistoric cliff
> ruins about a month ago, Palmer told Ranger Ed Alberts
> that he had camped as a child with his parents at
> Montezuma castle in the early spring of 1896, and that
> the party had excavated a burial at the point where the
> uppermost ladder now enters the ruin. The photograph
> of the ruins taken from the floor of the canyon is the
> clearest as to detail of any known early picture of the
> dwelling. It clearly shows a sealed-up doorway that was
> rediscovered by the custodian's wife a few years ago.

The photo of greater interest, though, was that of one of the
small mummies, photographed on a narrow ledge near the
castle's second floor on its eastern edge. "A close-up
photograph of the mummy shows it to be remarkably well-
preserved. Its probable age could only be determined by actual
examination," the paper said. "This is the second known
complete burial found at the castle and the only mummy found
there so far as the custodian knows."

Could it be that Montezuma Castle presents the best
evidence that the magical little people of the Southwest were
real? If that's the case, a spot associated with the mystical
Montezuma would seem to be a perfect one.

Chapter Notes

[1] Robinson, *Apache Voices*, p.184.

[2] I did find earlier articles from about twenty years before that seem to be
what the article was referring to. One, which amounted to only a small
blurb under "Territorial News" in the *Bisbee Cochise Review* of December
22, 1900, mentioned the finding of an "Aztec mummy" in the United
Verde mine. Oddly, some tried to claim, or perhaps just jest, that it was
the mummy of Emperor Montezuma himself!

MUMMY OF MONTEZUMA

The *Prescott Arizona Weekly Journal Miner* of December 12, 1900:

AN AZTEC MUMMY.

An Alleged Discovery of a Dried Up Pre-Historic Man at Jerome.

The Jerome News gives an extended account of the alleged finding of a mummy in the United Verde mine. The finding of a mummy is a possible thing, but this alleged discovery coming so closely on the heels of the finding of a bogus petrified man will make the story be received with a large portion of salt. After giving a very plausible account of the discovery of the News spoils the story by claiming it to be that of Montezuma, the Aztec Chief. The plausible story of the find as given in the News is as follows:

The finding of a mummified man by workmen at the United Verde m nes of Monday, December 3rd, created some little excitement in Jerome. The body is undoubtedly that of a man who, during life, was a giant, at least everything surrounding the find would signify that such was the case, as beside him was found a firearm somewhat similar to the shotgun used at the present time, but so large and of such weight that the average man today could not pose it for shooting. Beside the gun there were found near him working tools, all of which were manufactured of tempered copper, showing that the man must have been buried over 3,000 years ago—during the first age of copper. The body is well preserved but has evidently shriveled, yet many of the most important parts have undoubtedly remained their natural s ze.

"The numerous articles found with the body would signify that he was a king of some renown.

"The find was made in a cave exposed by the late caving in of the Verde mines. It was with woncer and awe that the workmen first entered the cave and handled the relics that must have been laid away centuries ago."

In 1737, another strange chapter unfolded in the legend of Montezuma. That year, a man named Agustín Ascuchul appeared, claiming to be a religious prophet who Montezuma had appeared to and anointed. Under this guise, Ascuchul influenced over 5,000 members of the Guaima and Pima tribes to follow him to a new home where they could worship Montezuma. The governor of Sonora, Juan Bautista de Anza, pictured in the portrait above, took this migration as a rebellion and sentenced Asuchul to death by hanging. Unfortunately, no more information than this is recounted per this Montezuma-induced migration. (Portrait by Fray Orci, c.1774)

14.
MONTEZUMA'S HEAD
Tales of Treasure

As stated before, Arizona has no less than five major landmarks bearing Montezuma's name, those being Montezuma Castle, the nearby Montezuma Well, and also Montezuma's Head. In the case of the latter, there are three different locations sharing the name Montezuma's Head. One lies in Maricopa County, another in Pima County, and yet another in Pinal County.

Not surprisingly, two out of the three Montezuma's Heads have a treasure legend associated with them. In Pinal County there is said to be a lost cache of gold accessible through a cave in the Star Mountains. Notably, Montezuma's Head—which did have a human profile—was not the location of the cave, just a major landmark on the way to it.

Far more interesting is the treasure of Maricopa County's Montezuma's Head. Like the other, it too bore a resemblance to a human head. A reporter for the *San Francisco Examiner* described it in this way:

> In the bluff of a solid rock at the southern end of a small and rugged range of treeless and barren mountains, running south from the Gila river for a distance of ten or twelve miles, is a distinctly outlined and perfectly formed image of a human head of immense proportions.[1]

The country of Montezuma's Head, AZ, according to an old postcard.

Of the reverence of the mountain, the article continued,

> There are a few remaining members of the once powerful race gathered together on the Gila river, where their descendants once resided, and are awaiting the time when the Great Spirit will release their good guardian and restore them to might and power and give them possession of the lands which are now occupied by the whites.

Purely legendary, the idea of the Great Spirit releasing their guardian referred to a myth that Montezuma himself had been turned to stone on the mountaintop and would one day revive. Thomas Penfield's book *Dig Here!* recounted the legend very well. Penfield began his discourse on the treasure with a brief overview of Montezuma:

> The legendary treasure of the New Mexico Indian god, Montezuma, is buried in at least a dozen places in the Southwest. To further complicate the matter, there are almost as many legends of the Aztec Montezuma's treasure buried in the same area of the United States.[2]

The story of the treasure of Montezuma's Head interestingly conjoined that of the mythical Montezuma with that of his real counterpart in Mexico. So the story went, Emperor Montezuma sent a treasure envoy northward to evade the hands of the conquistadors. In it was gold from the mines of Mexico. The envoy settled on Montezuma's Head, perhaps thinking the formation favored their leader. The gold was then sealed up in a cave somewhere on Montezuma's Head.

According to some variations, Montezuma himself escaped with the envoy. Upon reaching the mountain, Montezuma climbed its summit and turned to stone to guard the treasure. One day, when Montezuma's spirit returns from the East, it is said the stone statue will come to life. It will then walk down the mountain and open up the sealed treasure vault and redistribute the wealth to the indigenous peoples.

This belief was parroted in an article in the *Casa Grande Dispatch* of March 29, 1956, which stated:

> On the southern end of the Estrella Mountains is an out-cropping of granite that has the appearance of the face and head of an Indian. The Pimas believe it is a profile of their God, Montezuma. They further believe that he will awaken from his sleep some day, will gather all the brave and faithful around him, raise and lift his down-trodden people, and restore to his kingdom the old power and the glory, as it was before the Spaniards invaded Mexico.
>
> So strong is this belief that in parts of Old Mexico the Indians still keep fires constantly burning in anticipation of Montezuma's arrival.

Whether or not a stone Montezuma really rests upon the mountain, there is at least evidence of gold in the area. In the mid-1950s, the "yellowing skeleton of a prospector" was literally pushed out of the grave from an outgrowth of tree roots. The remains, encased inside an old redwood coffin, were discovered by a retired miner who lived near the Papago Reservation, and Montezuma's Head could be seen in the distance from the remains. "Nature, perhaps tired of its clandestine burden, had lifted the box on the roots of a sturdy tree and shoved it upward into the sunlight," reported the *Arizona Daily Star* of April 30, 1954. The man appeared to have been murdered by a blow to the head over fifty years before.

Desert Yields Murder Mystery

Pushed upward by a tree root until bared to the desert sun, the skull of this slain prospector seems to be staring in ghostly reproach at some unseen killer. (David Rees photo)

Arizona Daily Star (April 30, 1954).

The retired miner who found the remains was quoted as saying,

> I found a few chunks of rich gold ore that fellar maybe dug up somewhere around here 50 years ago. I think he was killed by someone who wanted his claim. I believe the killer buried that man here over his gold vein to keep it out of sight. I'm gonna dig that hole out until I locate that gold. It's got to be close by here somewhere."

Desert Yields Coffin, Bones of Slain Man

Dark board in trench is side of redwood coffin holding a murdered miner's corpse. The Palo Verde tree grew after his burial 50 years ago, sending its hungry roots down in a weird embrace around the flimsy casket. In background is Montezuma's head, an Indian landmark visible throughout the rugged desert area near Ajo.

Arizona Daily Star (April 30, 1954).

Perhaps the gold came from Montezuma's Head, and perhaps the murdered man was yet another victim of the curse of Montezuma ...

Chapter Notes

[1] Reprinted in *The Saint Paul Globe* of May 23, 1890.
[2] Penfield, *Dig Here!*, p.60.

Dr. Carlos Montezuma "Wassaja," c.1890.

15.
CHILD OF MONTEZUMA
Dr. Carlos Montezuma "Wassaja"

As stated several times before, there is an unfulfilled prophecy of Montezuma's return to bring prosperity and equality to the indigenous tribes of the Southwest. However, depending on one's perspective, perhaps it was partially fulfilled via an Apache man born in 1866.

In a 1905 letter to the Smithsonian Institute, Dr. Carlos Montezuma wrote, "I am a full-blooded Apache Indian, born around the year 1866... somewhere near Four Peaks, Arizona Territory..." Before he was a doctor, and furthermore, before he was called Montezuma, he was named "Wassaja," meaning *signaling* or *beckoning*. His parents comprised Chief Co-cu-ye-vah and his wife, Thil-ge-ya. One day in October of 1871, five-year-old Wassaja was captured by a Pima raiding party to serve as a child slave for barter.

The Pimas stopped at the mixed Anglo-Mexican village of Adamsville. As Wassaja's luck would have it, there at the time was Carlo Gentile, an Italian photographer chronicling the tribes of Arizona. Gentile took sympathy on Wassaja and purchased him for thirty silver dollars as a way of freeing him. Gentile then adopted the boy and renamed him Carlos Montezuma. The first name was after himself, but the surname Gentile chose because of his affinity for Montezuma Castle, and also the association of the Montezuma name with the indigenous peoples of Arizona at that time.

Carlo Gentile.

From 1872 to 1873, the father and son duo made ends meet by performing in a Chicago show entitled "The Scouts of the Prairie, and Red Deviltry As It Is!" at Nixon's Amphitheatre. Buffalo Bill headlined the show, and little Carlos was billed as "the young Apache captive, Azteka." Eventually, Gentile and Carlos settled in Chicago permanently, where the photographer opened a studio.

The future Dr. Montezuma alternated between public and homeschooling until he finally graduated with honors from Urbana High School in 1879. A child prodigy, he had enrolled for his first semester of college at only fourteen years old. At the University of Illinois, he studied everything from English to German, plus physiology, physics, physiology, mental science, microscopy, mineralogy, logic, constitutional history, political economy, geology, and zoology. Called Monte by his classmates at the university, he also took his first steps at being what we today call an activist. He gave a notable speech on Native American bravery, which was preserved in the May 5, 1883, edition of the campus paper, *The Illini*.

Dr. Carlos Montezuma. (University of Illinois Archives)

After graduating from the university in 1884, he notably began corresponding with Richard Henry Pratt, founder of the Carlisle Indian School in Pennsylvania. In 1887, at Pratt's invitation, Dr. Montezuma addressed audiences in New York and Philadelphia on the topic of Native American affairs and equality. Two years later, he received his doctorate of medicine from the Chicago Medical College. This made Dr. Carlos Montezuma the first Native American man to receive a medical degree.[1]

Following this, Dr. Montezuma spent several years practicing medicine on various reservations across North America. There he observed firsthand their often poor conditions, which fueled the fire in his fight for equality. In

1893, his adopted father, Carlo Gentile, passed away and Dr. Montezuma helped to financially support his widowed step-mother. For a time, he even fostered his little brother, Carlos Gentile Jr., until he moved to California with his mother in 1896. That same year, Dr. Montezuma opened his own private practice in Chicago.

In 1901, he returned to Arizona, where he reconnected with his long-lost relatives that he had not seen since he was abducted by the Pima raiders. Seeing how his people loved their ancestral lands, he fought for the creation of the Fort McDowell Yavapai/Mohave-Apache Reservation, formed late in 1903. The next year, Dr. Montezuma founded the Indian Fellowship League, which was the first urban Indian organization in the U.S. and located in Chicago.

Confident due to past victories, Dr. Montezuma became more aggressive in his quest for Native American rights, speaking out more boldly against the U.S. government's treatment of Native Americans on reservations. To that end, he helped to found the Society of American Indians in 1911, which became the first Indian rights organization. In 1916 came the monthly magazine *Wassaja*, which he used as a means of educating readers on the ineptitudes of the Bureau of Indian affairs, the education system, and other matters.

Gravely ill with tuberculosis, Dr. Montezuma passed away on January 31, 1923, in Arizona and was buried at the Fort McDowell Indian cemetery. While he may not have come on the wings of a giant eagle, Dr. Montezuma hailed from the East just as the prophecy foretold, and he did a great deal not just for his own tribe, but all the indigenous tribes of North America, and in his own way, perhaps fulfilled a "second coming" of Montezuma.

Chapter Notes

[1] Susan La Flesche Picotte, also Native American, was the first the same year in 1889.

PART IV

**Montezuma elsewhere
in New Mexico**

"Although tolerating in their pueblo the church of the cross, and occasional visits of a Christian priest, [the Puebloans] seem to have little regard for the Catholic religion. In secret they glory in loyalty to Montezuma. They endeavor to keep their Spanish neighbors ignorant of their ceremonies, but say that Americans are brothers of the children of Montezuma, and their friends; therefore they hide from them neither their sacred dances in the courts, nor the midnight meetings of the caciques in the estufa. Beneath the apparent multiplicity of gods these Indians have a firm faith in the Deity, the unseen Spirit of Good. His name is above all things sacred, and, like Jehovah of the Jews, too holy to be spoken. Montezuma is his son and their King. The sun, moon and stars are His works worthy of their adoration."—
Lieutenant Amiel Weeks Whipple,
via The Oroville Weekly Butte Record
of October 9, 1858.

16.

MONTEZUMA AT ACOMA
Legends of Sky City

S econd to Pecos, the New Mexico pueblo most associated with Montezuma is Sky City at Acoma. As the oldest continually inhabited ancestral village in North America, Acoma Pueblo has a great deal of mystique. This is predominantly because the village is situated atop a 365-foot-tall mesa about 60 miles west of Albuquerque. However, in addition to its unique placement making it noteworthy, the pueblo has many memorable legends. Amidst tales of Hero Twins, witches, magical paintings, and flying horses were also stories of the great Montezuma, notably that he was born at Acoma.

The *Inter Ocean* of August 22, 1897, claimed that

The historic pueblo of Acoma is most directly connected with Montezuma and his acts, because it is said that he was born on this spot. It is true that this honor is claimed by many other pueblos, and consequently this central figure of the olden time in our southwestern territory has come to be regarded as a species of "composite photograph"—the crystallization of the characteristics of many noble men into a type which came to be regarded with veneration, and eventually deified...[1]

MYTH OF THE MESA

A Daring Princeton Professor Proclaims Its Disenchantment.

AZTEC MYSTERY PROBED

A Mighty Rock Ingeniously Scaled with Rope and Chair.

No Signs Upon Its Top That the Red Man Ever Made It His Impregnable Home.

There is no more interesting study than that of the myths of the ancient inhabitants of this continent. Prominent among them are the stories which center around Montezuma—the Moses of the Aztecs.

The historic pueblo of Acoma is most directly connected with Montezuma and his acts, because it is said that he was born on this spot. It is true that this honor is claimed by many other pueblos, and consequently this central figure of the olden time in our southwestern territory has come to be regarded as a species of "composite photograph"—the crystallization of the characteristics of many noble men into a type which came to be regarded with veneration, and eventually deified —for he became their prophet, priest, and first ruler.

Descended from such a remote period comes the medicine man's myth, for such it turns

The *Inter Ocean* of August 22, 1897.

San Esteban del Ray of Acoma Pueblo.

The *Inter Ocean* continued their tales of Montezuma at Acoma with repeats of the eternal flame and the sacred tree:

Montezuma taught them the arts and manufactures which distinguish these tribes from their nomadic brethren of the plains. He gave them the primitive religious ideas which even today exercise a certain

127

influence over their lives. In spite of the Christian ideas which have slowly been introduced among them by the devoted men and women who have passed their lives at these isolated posts of duty and privilege. He told them that a race of conquerors and oppressors would subdue them after he had disappeared, and he planted a tree, which they were to watch while they cared for the sacred fire which he started. When the tree fell deliverance from their enemies should come from the East, and that would be the beginning of an era of plenty, abundant rains, and prosperity.

Acoma Pueblo - The Sky City

One tradition went that vandalizing of sacred petroglyphs near Acoma would result in Montezuma striking down the perpetrators with lightning according to the *Oroville Weekly Butte Record* of October 9, 1858.

If the *Inter Ocean* actually got these stories from someone at Acoma, or if they simply transposed them from Pecos to Acoma is unknown. In any case, the article claimed that like at Pecos and elsewhere, the Acomans watched every morning for Montezuma's return on the wings of his great eagle: "Like all other Pueblos, Acoma still bows to the sun-god, and still awaits the return of Montezuma as the Jews wait the coming of Messiah."

Like the footprints at Pecos, Montezuma, too, left his literal mark at Acoma. The *Catholic Advance* column, entitled "Stray Bits" by William Schaefers, of May 25, 1929, detailed the marks of Montezuma at Acoma, which they called "the Cathedral on the Desert."

> We quickly hop into our car and begin the steep, treacherous descent down the mesa side. It is rough and rocky going. We pass a rock that crowns a little knoll, and perceive that its flat surface carries the imprint of human toes. What is it? Montezuma's Toes! The Indians declare that from this particular rock their god, Montezuma, ascended into the heavens and that on leaving this earth he left behind him the imprint of his toes on this rock.[2]

Montezuma was also associated with a popular Acoma legend, that being that of nearby Katzimo Mesa. According to the Acomans, the steep 430-foot-high mesa was their original home until a great storm destroyed their only approach. Though nineteenth century academics scoffed at this notion, an 1897 ascent by Frederick Webb Hodge, an archaeologist for the Smithsonian, found evidence of habitation in the form of arrowheads and other objects.

The story went that one fateful day, all of the pueblo save for three women and a boy had ventured into the valley below to work the fields. The three women had been too ill to go to work that day, and so a youth named A-chi-te stayed behind to look after them. It was the summer monsoon season, and a catastrophic cloudburst struck the mesa so hard that it made some of the adobe dwellings crumble. In the chaos, A-chi-te pulled his mother from the rubble of their home and then decided to brave the hurricane-force winds down the mesa to get help. As he did, the crushing torrent caused the great rock ladder leading up the mesa to fall and shatter into pieces. As it was, the stone ladder's "base stood on a great hill of sand,"[3] hence how the intense rainfall eroded it away so swiftly.

The poor Acomans later tried in vain to scale the cliff not just to return to their old home but to rejoin the three women now stranded atop the great rock. Early-day historian Charles Lummis told the papers, "The three women imprisoned above were seen for a long time. One, crazed by grief, flung herself off the cliff; the others finally starved."[4]

Photo of Enchanted Mesa taken from Acoma Pueblo by W.H. Jackson in 1899.

Some say sacrifices were made to a deity of some sort in hopes of returning to the top of the mesa, but they were all in vain. "The spirits of those who died are still hovering over the 'Mesa Encantada' where they are destined to remain until Montezuma comes again to earth," one article dramatically concluded.[5]

Chapters Notes

[1] Likewise, the *Kansas City Journal* of October 27, 1880, held that Montezuma was born at Acoma before relocating to Pecos.

[2] That particular route up the mesa is apparently known as Montezuma Trail.

[3] Lummis, *A New Mexico David*, p.51.

[4] *Montana Helena Independent* (August 13, 1897), p.2.

[5] Ibid.

17.
IDOL OF MONTEZUMA
Montezuma at Laguna Pueblo

Very near Acoma is Laguna Pueblo. The two settlements share a common language, and currently, a joint high school. Being located in the same vicinity, the two have held a form of rivalry over the years as well. A good example of this was the case of a painting of Saint Joseph. Legend had it that it was brought to Acoma by Fray Ramirez, the first priest to be stationed there permanently, in the 1700s. Laguna Pueblo, however, was envious, as they felt the painting was enchanted and, therefore, somehow blessed the crops of the Acomans.

In the early 1800s, the painting vanished from Acoma and ended up at Laguna. Perhaps not coincidentally, the crops of Laguna Pueblo began to prosper while Acoma's suffered. The Acomans marched to Laguna to reclaim what some considered a magic talisman only to be repelled by armed guards at the door of Laguna's chapel. Conditions worsened at Acoma until a local priest involved with both churches intervened. Basically, he suggested a "divine" method of drawing lots. Blank slips of paper would be placed in two baskets at the feet of a statue of Saint Joseph. Both baskets also contained one paper with the likeness of the saint. A representative of Acoma would draw from their basket, while a representative of Laguna would do the same. Whoever drew the saint first would get the painting. Acoma won, but Laguna refused to yield.

San Jose de Laguna Mission Church & Convento by James M. Slack (February 27, 1934).

When New Mexico was acquired as a territory of the United States, the case was taken to the Territorial Supreme Court in 1857, which ruled in Acoma's favor. When the Acomans jubilantly marched to Laguna to reclaim their painting, they found it midway there propped up under a pinon tree. The supernaturally-minded thought the painting may have materialized there by itself, but the more practical understood the Laguna peoples simply didn't wish to witness the triumph of Acoma in regaining the painting. Today the faded painting hangs in San Esteban del Rey.

Even though Laguna lost the painting, they may have possessed something even more valuable in the form of an idol of Montezuma. In fact, it's the only pueblo recorded as having one, which is rather unusual. The tale of the idol of Montezuma surfaced thanks to U.S. Attorney W.W.H. Davis, who visited Laguna Pueblo in 1855 along with his family. He gave a detailed account of the incident in his book, *El Gringo*:

> To the present day the Indians of Laguna worship an object they call by the name of the Aztec king, and which is fashioned to resemble him, as they suppose. They keep up the estufa because, as they say, it was instituted

132

by Montezuma, and, as far as I have been able to learn, they still number the sun among the objects of their heathen worship.[1]

William Watts Harts Davis from "A collection of papers read before the Bucks County Historical Society." Davis was naturally confused by Lacuna Pueblo's association with Montezuma and the Aztec race in general. Davis consulted with the great German explorer Baron Alexander von Humboldt, who had toured Mexico and the Southwest fifty years earlier. Humboldt assured him that the Puebloans spoke an entirely different language than the Aztecs and also noted that "the Indians of New Mexico were entirely unknown to the people of Southern Mexico."[2]

While in Laguna, Davis asked his young guide if he might be permitted to gaze upon this mysterious effigy of Montezuma to see what, if any, resemblance it bore to the great Aztec King. Davis was naturally unaware of the Montezuma myth of the pueblos not being a native of the region, and he must have been confused at the sight of the idol. The young man led him and his companions to the house where the idol was kept, with Davis writing that it was "the most cherished, and probably the only one still retained of all their ancient heathen gods."[3]

Laguna Pueblo c. 1879.

Davis was either told, or possibly he just presumed, that the figure was brought forth in periods of drought to help invoke the rain, "but whether it has ever been able to bring refreshing showers to the parched earth is a question open to discussion."[4]

Davis and his companions ascended a ladder to gain entrance to what he described as a "small and badly-lighted room, where we found a shriveled-up old Indian, entirely naked, except a small cloth about his loins and moccasins upon the feet."[5] After their young guide assured the man that his companions were not officials from the Mexican government who would try and abscond with their idol, the old man and an "old hag of a woman who had come in in the meantime" conferred and agreed to let the newcomers look upon their idol.[6]

Woman from Laguna Pueblo. (Library of Congress)

After a few minutes, the elderly woman returned carrying something in an old cloth, which she carefully placed on the floor and unfolded. Davis described it thusly:

I had expected to see something in imitation of man or beast, but there was presented to our sight an object that neither resembled any thing upon the earth, in the heavens above, or in the sea beneath, and I felt that it could hardly be sinful in the poor ignorant Indians to fall down and worship it. The god Montezuma is made of tanned skin of some sort, and the form is circular, being about nine inches in height, and the same in diameter. The top is covered with the same material, but the lower end is open, and one half is painted red, and the other green. Upon the green side is fashioned the rude representation of a man's face. Two oblong apertures in the skin, in the shape of right-angled triangles, with the bases inward, are the eyes; there is no nose, and a circular piece of leather, fastened about two inches below the eyes, represents the mouth; and two similar pieces, one on each side, opposite the outer corners of the eyes, are intended for the ears. This completes the *personnel* of the god, with the addition of a small tuft of leather upon the top, which is dressed with feathers when it is brought out to be worshiped upon public days.[7]

Davis then proceeded to describe the behavior of the Laguna people towards the object:

The three Indians present looked upon it with the greatest apparent veneration, who knelt around it in the most devout manner, and went through a form of prayer, while one of the number sprinkled upon it a white powder. Mateo, the Indian who accompanied us, spoke in praise of Montezuma, and told us that it was God, and the brother of God. After contemplating this singular spectacle for a few minutes, we withdrew, quite astonished at what we had seen. Who would have believed that within the limits of our Union, in the middle of the nineteenth century, there was to be found such a debased form of heathen worship?[8]

Presumably, Davis eventually learned of the strange, conjoined history of Montezuma and the pueblo deity of Poseyemu. Whether he did or not, Davis thankfully did his part to illuminate Montezuma's enigmatic presence in the Southwest.

Chapter Notes

[1] Davis, *El Gringo*, p.130.
[2] Ibid, p.131.
[3] Ibid, p.395.
[4] Ibid.
[5] Ibid.
[6] This being 1855 was shcrtly after Mexican rule had ended. In fact, no one of the Mexican race was even permitted to so much as look at the idol according to Davis.
[7] Davis, *El Gringo*, p.396.
[8] Ibid.

Zuni Pueblo in western New Mexico, shown above, was reported to have Montezuma legends according to the *Richmond Dispatch* of May 20, 1880. It reported that

These Zunis are undoubtedly Aztecs, descendants of the princely Montezumas. A myth is current among them closely allied to the Jewish belief in the return of the Savior. According to tradition Montezuma was carried away upon an eagle's back, some time to return in the same manner to restore the pristine glories of the race. Therefore the eagle is considered sacred. The Zunis, like the ancient Persians, are fire-worshippers, and popular tradition affirms that in their "estufa" a sacred fire-emblem of the sun is kept constantly burning, guarded by twelve priests, to prevent the possibility of extinction.

18.
MONTEZUMA AT TAOS
Yet Another Birthplace for Montezuma

In addition to Pecos and Acoma, Montezuma also had strong ties to Taos Pueblo. For instance, some stories went that Taos was the first pueblo founded by Montezuma, followed by Acoma and Pecos.[1] Along those same lines, a nearby mountain was said to be a treasure house of Montezuma's as well. Another account even had the sacred flame transported from Pecos to Taos for safekeeping. Via W.E. Curtis, the *Las Vegas Daily Gazette* of April 29, 1883, reported that as more and more travelers passed by on the Santa Fe Trail, the Pecos Indians became concerned that "the impious" would extinguish the eternal flame and therefore prevent Montezuma's return. As such, "they took it one day with great ceremony over the mountains to the pueblo of Taos, where, according to tradition, Montezuma's eagle first alighted in his flight from Pecos." As far as Curtis understood, the eternal flame burned in a secret temple in Taos, well-guarded from unbelievers who might prevent Montezuma's return.[2]

The boldest claim of Taos Pueblo, though, was that Montezuma was born there. How the author of the article about to be quoted got their information, and if it's even remotely correct, is unknown, but the *Los Angeles Times* of December 10, 1885, claimed that Montezuma was "born at the pueblo of Teguayo—which is generally understood to mean Taos…"

According to the story that followed, during a time of great famine, the Great Spirit gifted a young maiden three pinon nuts for she and her grandmother. When the virgin ate one of the nuts, she miraculously became pregnant, and eventually, Montezuma was born. "The boy was held of little account in his native village. He was poor, ugly, dirty, careless, ragged, and a vagabond," the *Times* said. Everything changed upon the death of the tribal shaman. When the elders couldn't agree on a successor, they deferred to the young men of the pueblo, who came up with the idea of casting lots. As it so happened, this resulted in the most unlikely choice of all, that being Montezuma:

[Montezuma] told the derisive multitude that he had been commissioned from on high to be their leader; and in proof, promised that upon the next grand hunt he would lead them, and that they should catch rabbits, quail and ducks in their hands, while the antelopes, mountain sheep, black-tailed deer, bears and cougars should voluntarily come in and surrender.

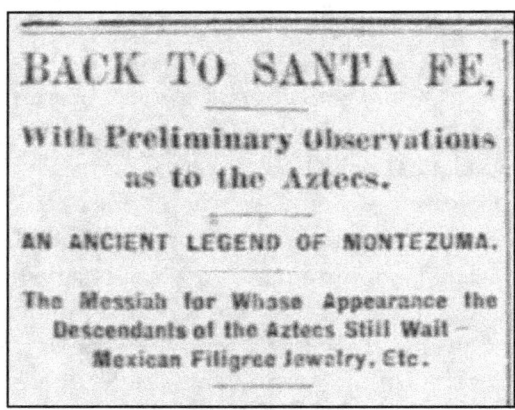

The *Los Angeles Times* of December 10, 1885.

The night before the hunt, Montezuma tossed and turned on his sheepskin bed, wondering how he would realize the bold claims he made the day before. At that moment, the Great Spirit appeared before him and told him to take the blanket and the moccasins that his mother left him at her death and to fear not. Montezuma went to his mother's house as instructed and found the moccasins, which were inlaid with precious turquoise. He also found a strong bow made of mezquit wood, a cougar-skinned quiver full of arrows, and a headdress trimmed with eagle feathers. Lastly, he found a sacred rattle made from the hooves of several wild animals.

Taos Pueblo. (Library of Congress)

Alone, Montezuma sounded the rattle in the four cardinal directions, and this signaled to the animals that they were to surrender to him. After this, Montezuma appeared before his people and they were shocked at his stately appearance, wondering how it could be the same man. The hunt proceeded as promised, with birds being caught in the hunters' hands. A procession of deer and antelope came willingly to the group at the sound of Montezuma's rattle. Montezuma won the favor of his people that day, but his story wasn't over yet. Another challenge came when Montezuma prophesied a great rain. Though the story bore a few similarities to that of Noah's, the flood wasn't to be apocalyptic. The massive rains were to be good for the land to make it fertile for crops, but it would also wash away the less sturdy dwellings. The faithful fortified their homes, while the scoffers did not. When the heavy rain came, the doubters "perished under the falling walls of their adobes."

Eventually, the Great Spirit called Montezuma to move on to the south. Before he did so, Montezuma chose a bride in the form of Malinche, a beautiful maiden from Zuni Pueblo. With Malinche as his queen, Montezuma boarded "a great dark eagle" that had flown down from the sun. Montezuma and Malinche mounted their "living throne" and flew away to the unknown regions of the south. Some of the tribe stayed in Taos, but others followed the great eagle from the ground. Over the next several years, the eagle would land at a certain spot, Montezuma and Malinche would establish a new pueblo, and then move on. Some would stay behind, while others would again follow, eventually all the way to Mexico, where the Aztec Empire was founded.

The article concluded that in Taos, "the faithful Pueblos are watching expectantly today for the shadow of the great eagle to fall across their houses, or for the rush of his mighty wings to sound in their ears."

However, according to Alice Bullock in her book *Mountain Villages*, Montezuma routinely returns to the hot springs near Taos once a year at Ojo Caliente. Bullock related, "[Montezuma], it is said, still returns one day each year, however, to visit his grandmother who lives in the pool where the 'green springs' bubble up."[3] Therefore, Taos holds the distinction of being the only pueblo Montezuma returns to.

Chapter Notes

[1] The history of Montezuma as presented in the *Oroville Weekly Butte Record* of October 9, 1858, went that he was born at Acoti. According to this iteration, Taos was the first pueblo he founded, followed by Acoma, then Pecos. From there he went to Mexico, where he lived until the Spanish came. Rather than dying during Cortés's invasion, he simply disappeared was and hoped to one day return. This view held that even the enemies of the pueblos, that being the Navajo and the Apache, were descended from Montezuma.

[2] Validating this, perhaps, was an article in the *South Haven Daily Tribune* of April 2, 1906, which claimed the eternal flame still burned in a labyrinth hidden beneath Taos Pueblo as well.

[3] Bullock, *Mountain Villages*, p.101. Note: Bullock called Montezuma by his traditional name of "Pose-Yemo," though.

19.

THE SERPENT AT TAOS
Another Fate for the Snake

Earlier was recounted the legend and lore of the giant snake rumored to exist somewhere near Pecos. As it turns out, it wasn't the only one. In 1910, New Mexico Folklorist Aurelio Espinosa spoke to the subject of human sacrifice and pueblo serpents, or "Monster Vipers," in his piece on New Mexico folklore. Interestingly, he singled out Taos as the home of a giant serpent rather than Pecos.

This is a Spanish-Indian myth. The belief is that the Pueblo Indians of New Mexico have in each pueblo a monster viper (*el víborón*) in a large subterranean cave, which is nourished with seven living children every year. I know absolutely nothing about the origin of this myth, and have had no time to study it; but I am inclined to believe that this is a pure Indian myth, probably of Aztec origin. The interesting thing about it is, that the Indians themselves have very vague ideas concerning it, some even denying it. The belief among the New Mexicans of this Indian myth is widespread, and the gradual disappearance of the New Mexico Pueblo Indians is explained by the myth in question. In the pueblo of Taos it is said that an Indian woman, when her turn came to deliver her child to the monster viper, fled to her Mexican neighbors, and thus saved her child.[1]

That last bit was likely a repeat of the story related by Mariano Ruíz's grandson to Edward S. Curtis in 1924. Presumably, Espinosa heard the story, or some variation of it, and transposed it to Taos for some reason.

That said, stories of a sacred serpent at Taos did exist. In his seminal *Witchcraft in the Southwest*, Mark Simmons recorded that "Hispanos living in the vicinity of Taos Pueblo once believed the Indians of that village harbored a divine snake."[2] Simmons got his information from *Shadows of the Past* by Cleofas Jaramillo, which gave a firsthand account of life in northern New Mexico's mountain villages. It was through Jaramillo that the serpent was linked to Taos:

> Beyond La Glorieta, the picnic grounds of the Taos people, the Indians forbade white people to enter the River Canyon. Stories were told about the Indians having an enchanted gold mine in the mountains; others about the Indians having a *biboron* (monster rattlesnake), to which they fed infant babies on certain feast days, and this was the reason for the non—increase of the pueblo's population.
>
> During the Indian and Spanish uprising against the American occupation, and while the United States

soldiers were bombarding the pueblo church, where the natives had fixed their stronghold, the *biboron* was being moved to safety from the north pueblo to the south side across the river, on a hand-cart covered with blankets. The Indian who braved the shower of missiles, in order to save the idol, dropped wounded, as he reached the mouth of the kiva; he dragged the monster wrapped in blankets down the ladder, only to drop dead at the bottom of the kiva.[3]

Since some stories held that the eternal flame was taken to Taos, and considering what Jaramillo related, perhaps the sacred snake went along with it?

Chapter Notes

[1] Espinosa, "New-Mexican Spanish Folk-Lore," *Journal of American Folklore* Vol. 23, No. 90 (Oct. - Dec., 1910), p.403.

[2] Simmons, *Witchcraft in the Southwest*, Kindle Edition.

[3] Jaramillo, *Shadows of the Past*, pp.43-44. It's possible that Jaramillo accidentally transposed the Pecos story to Taos, though it should be noted that Taos does have a north and south pueblo, so the description of the location better matches Taos than Pecos.

SPIRITUAL SERPENT

In a broader sense, outside of Pecos, rather than a literal giant snake, Montezuma's serpent was sometimes a spectral creature that appeared to grant wisdom if one were to either kiss its tongue or place their head in its open mouth as a sign of their devotion.[1] Such an account was given firsthand to authors Sherry Hansen-Steiger and Brad Steiger, in their book *Montezuma's Serpent and Other Supernatural Tales of the Southwest*. A man identified as Reuben Montoya related that back in 1940, he lived in an unidentified New Mexico village with "much talk of witches and devils."[2]

Montoya and his grandfather were walking through an arroyo at night when a gigantic rattlesnake materialized in front of them. Montoya remembered that it was as tall as his grandfather when it reared up and as big around as a large man's thy. It came before Reuben and touched him with his tongue. Though young Reuben was unaware, the serpent was offering its tongue for him to kiss. Eventually the snake disappeared in a puff of smoke, with a smell of "spent shotgun shells" and Reuben's grandfather began to weep. He told the boy that he had rejected an offer of wisdom and power from the serpent of Montezuma. The angry grandfather slapped his grandson and the boy ran home in tears.

Montoya's mother consoled him, explaining that his caution was not totally unwarranted, as sometimes the Devil could appear as the sacred serpent to trick "vain and ambitious men."[3] She advised him to be ready if Montezuma's sacred serpent appeared to him again in the future. At the age of 22, Montoya conducted a seven-day fast and encountered the sacred serpent again in a vision. Afterwards, Montoya became a healer. As stated before, this was not presented as a folktale, but Montoya's honest experience.

Section Notes

---

[1] Kissing a snake's tongue was notably also a part of the Spanish rendition of the witches' sabbat, wherein practitioners did so to obtain wisdom.

[2] Steiger, *Montezuma's Serpent*, p.1.

[3] Ibid, p.2.

20.

TAOS TREASURE
Curse of Montezuma

Acommon legend across the Southwest is that of Montezuma's lost treasure. There are many variations of it, but it typically went that during the fall of the Aztec Empire, Montezuma sent a treasure envoy northwards to hide precious gold and other treasures from the conquerors. As such, any mysterious treasure cache of unknown origin, from those at Victorio Peak to the Superstition Mountains, has been speculated to have come from Montezuma.

A good example of the general story was given in an article appearing in the *Gold!* almanac of 1969 by Carl Howe. Howe related that Montezuma's successor, Guatomozin, sent a procession of riches northward to escape the Spaniards. According to Howe's article:

> This fabulous treasure was entrusted to the High Priest, who supervised its transfer to secret hiding places in the mountains. According to the legend, the treasure bearing slaves traveled in a northwesterly direction for many moons and then came to a mountain on the edge of a desert. There, in that gloomy, desolate place, the treasure was hidden and the slaves put to death and buried with the treasure. A curse was put upon the treasure and the mountain itself–a curse to be promptly invoked were the treasure ever to be molested.[1]

Although Howe was trying to correlate Arizona's Lost Dutchman treasure to Montezuma, a better candidate for the location might be the highest point in New Mexico: Wheeler Peak. Formerly known as Taos Peak, this was not only the spot where Montezuma's treasure was stored, but it was also where he would one day reappear according to the beliefs of Taos Pueblo.

Similar to the treasure procession story related by Carl Howe, it was said that after the Aztecs had safely secured the treasure within Taos Peak, nearly all members of the procession were executed. According to Howard Bryan's "Off the Beaten Path" column, "The leaders of the expedition then executed the rank and file members and buried them in a common grave near the hidden treasure. The leaders then returned to Mexico City, their lips sealed."[2]

McAVOY HILL, DESCENDING INTO MORENO VALLEY, SHOWING WHEELER PEAK OF SANGRE DE CRISTO RANGE.

SCENIC HIGHWAY BETWEEN TAOS AND RATON, N. M.

Notably, it was the roving actor/journalist Matt Field who gave the most elaborate telling of the treasure of Taos Peak. (If you'll recall, it was also Field who gave the most romantic recounting of the legend of the eternal flame.) Field's description of Taos Peak, which he mistakenly called "Toas Peak," is worth reprinting:

Like the spirit itself of some fabled Genii enchained among the rocky hills, appears that enormous pile known as the mountain of Toas. A perpetual gloom hangs round it through day as well as night, and even when the sun is brightest, it assumes no livelier appearance, but seems ever to be involved in shadow. When a storm gathers, the lofty peak of this mountain is soon hidden, and the heavy laden clouds roll down the dark sides as though poured forth from a crater at its summit. The voice of the storm seems to rumble within its breast, and the inhabitants of the valley peep from their dwellings at the black mountain, with fear, and curiosity and wonder.[3]

Field learned from locals that supposedly due to the mountain's enchanted nature, anyone who attempted to scale it, "became lunatics, and could never tell what they had seen."[4] Field continued that, "This fact spread great alarm and awe among the people, and the opinion was soon entertained that the black mountain was the spot chosen by Montezuma for his reappearance." After this belief was established, people steered clear of the summit. All that is but "a wealthy young Spaniard" from Mexico City who was visiting the region. His visit occurred "many, very many years ago," according to Field, who himself toured the area in the 1840s.[5]

As all fairytale characters are wont to do, the young man from Mexico City laughed at the superstitions of the natives and dared to climb their sacred mountain. Despite warnings from the locals, he ascended the mountain "followed by a crowd of the most daring spirits of the valley."[6] By way of climbing up "a splintered crag,"[7] the young man crept across a deep, snow-filled chasm known to have taken the lives of several men before him. Eventually, he reached the narrow ledge at the summit and disappeared from view. With his ax, he began working holes in the ice until he broke into an immense cavern.

Calling to his companions from inside, the man claimed that he had made a magnificent discovery that would "astonish the world." The young man described "a magnificent cavern, through which ran inexhaustible veins of gold, and lit into the blaze of day with the glare of precious stones."[8] He claimed that the interior of the mountain was hollow and that it was "one immense cavern, down which, from the entrance, ran winding galleries of easy dissent, leading to various brilliant apartments." He beseeched his companions to follow him and see for themselves, lest no one believe them when they returned.

However, the spirit of the mountain would not have it. Field explained:

Scarcely had this announcement left the lips of the speaker when a whirlwind came shrieking around the mountain peak, and the young man was seen to fall upon his face, and cling to the edge of the rock to preserve himself from being blown over the precipice. The terrified people called to him to descend instantly; but the sky darkened, and a thunderbolt suddenly struck the pinnacle by which he had ascended, which fell with a frightful roar into the deep cleft, and his retreat was cut off forever. Filled with consternation and terror the people fled away down the mountainside, abandoning the wretched victim to his fate, and shutting their ears against his screams for assistance… The reckless young Mexican was never heard of more; and this is the legend told and believed by the simple people of the valley, of the black mountain of Toas, and the cavern of Montezuma's Treasure.[9]

What the original version of this tale was like is anyone's guess, but it's likely that Field greatly exaggerated it.

Chapter Notes

[1] Howe, *Gold!*, p.41..

[2] Bryan, "Off the Beaten Path," clipping, n.d. In the same column, Bryan also noted that the nearby, "Blue Lake, apparently, is steeped in Montezuma legends." Unfortunately, he didn't elaborate.

[3] *Matt Field on the Santa Fe Trail*, p.184.

[4] Ibid, p.185.

[5] Ibid.

[6] Ibid, p.186.

[7] Ibid.

[8] Ibid.

[9] Ibid, pp.186-187.

The Montezuma, HOT SPRINGS, NEW MEXICO

OWNED AND OPERATED BY THE

Santa Fé Route.

21.

MONTEZUMA CASTLE
Million-Dollar Resort of the West

Located six miles northwest of Las Vegas is the little settlement of Montezuma, nestled in Gallinas Canyon.[1] There also is the imposing structure of Montezuma Castle. Not to be confused with the Arizona cliff-dwellings, it was constructed in the 1880s and looks as though it would be right at home in the English countryside, having been built in the Queen Ann style. The Montezuma was one of the first million-dollar resorts of the West which was built, owned, and operated by the Santa Fe Railroad. Construction began in 1881 and was completed the next year. Preceding that, it was simply the site of the hot springs, yet another of Montezuma's alleged birthplaces. According to F. Stanley in his *Montezuma New Mexico Story*, the Pecos peoples considered the area their "particular place of worship."[2] Stanley continued,

> They had a cult and ritual as early as 800 AD. Legend reveals that they were led to the spot by a deer. Eventually other pueblos sought the curative waters so that the Salinas, Piros and neighboring tribes were restricted to specified times that all would have an opportunity to use the springs. This natural hot water was a thing of mystery for the aborigines, and it is said that no man or animal was hunted there, for it was a sanctuary. No man was an enemy so long as he stayed at the springs.[3]

An article by Pearl Stanford recounted the more magical aspects of the springs as well:

> Legend says that long before the coming of the white man the present site of the hotel was the meeting place for many Indian tribes who used the curative waters of its numerous hot springs. Making yearly treks over the mountains and from the plains, they brought their old and their sick to bathe in the healing waters.[4]

Photograph of the Hot Springs of Montezuma, taken by James N. Furlong sometime in the late 1870s.

Some rumors and stories hold that an ancient pueblo was established in the area, but no ruins of such have ever been verified. And, somehow or another, the hot springs became one of Montezuma's many birthplaces in New Mexico. Stanley attributed this rumor to General Kearny's occupation of the area in the Mexican-American War, writing,

> Out of their visit the legend of Montezuma and his days in New Mexico are said to have made the rounds in the American press. They maintained that Pecos Indians believed that Montezuma was trained here [at the hot springs] in his duties as king until carried off to Mexico by an eagle to found his empire.[5]

First Montezuma Hotel & Bathhouse, c.1881-1884, photographed by James N. Furlong.

Stanford's article, "Fabulous Montezuma" appearing in *True West*, offered another Pecos-based alteration of the legend of Montezuma. Rather than departing on the back of an eagle as so many held, according to Stanford, Montezuma had been killed in a battle of some sort near Pecos. She added,

> Being a gentle and trusting people, they were sure their beloved chief had just disappeared into the clouds which hovered over their native mountains, and that he would return to them in a far distant age, clad in garments of glory.[6]

The subject of Stanford's article was not really Montezuma himself, but the magnificent hotel that bore his name. Though a resort had been constructed at the hot springs, the Adobe Hotel operated by Thomas Moore and his wife, in the late 1870s, a more magnificent structure was later erected by the Santa Fe Railroad company. This was, of course, the magnificent Montezuma Castle.

Construction began in 1881 at a cost of $200,000 and was completed in 1882. The finished structure boasted 270 rooms, all elegantly furnished in the Queen Ann style, and the hotel was able to host 300 guests. Steel engravings adorned the walls throughout the complex. The dining room could

155

accommodate 100 and spanned forty by seventy feet. Above the heads of the diners hung eight gas-lit chandeliers. Axminster carpets lined the floors—2,500 yards worth in fact. For entertainment, the hotel sported four bowling lanes, and outside, archery and croquet could be played on the grassy grounds.

On the night of April 17, 1882, a tour deforce grand opening was held. Over four hundred guests were on scene to toast to The Montezuma's opening. In the words of F. Stanley:

> Practically every blue-blood east and west of the Mississippi arrived for opening night. Glamour, glitter, and glass moved like actors on a stage. If the [nearby Gallinas River] dried up that night it might have been re-filled and re-flooded with all the fine drinks that emptied into the bidden and unbidden of Montezuma's opening night.[7]

Dinner lasted from six to eight p.m. and the guests reportedly danced 'til dawn to the music of the Fourth Cavalry orchestra from Fort Union.[8] In attendance was a who's who of society such as Fred Harvey, who served as the main speaker. Of note per the myth of Montezuma were the opening remarks given by Las Vegas resident Don Miguel Otero. Don Otero recounted the legend of the mythical Montezuma, claiming he was born at the nearby hot springs before alighting on an eagle to found the Aztec Empire. Don Otero naturally also recounted the prophecy of his return and made the bold statement that the current Montezuma hotel had accomplished this in some way, as he declared, "Tonight we hail his coming in the new and splendid halls of Montezuma."

The remains of the second Montezuma after the fire of August 8, 1885.

Following this came a boast from the hotel's engineer, M. Dinsmore of Boston, who boldly claimed it was impossible for the Montezuma to burn, seeing that it had the most up-to-date fire alarms and water pumps. In a way, the hotel was a bit like the *Titanic*—ahead of its time for luxury and destined for destruction. Interestingly, the hotel has burned to the ground and been rebuilt no less than three times, making it not unlike the Phoenix—a monicker the Montezuma briefly bore.

On the night of January 18, 1884, the hotel caught flame. By the time the fire department arrived on scene, it was too late to save the massive structure. Instead, the firefighters took to saving the bottles of liquor from the cellar and drank the night away while a "Nero-minded individual produced an accordion, sat on a hill, and played to his heart's content"[9] as the Montezuma burned. Luckily, no one was killed.

The Montezuma rose from its ashes a little over a year later, appropriately rechristened The Pheonix, though the name didn't last long and it reverted to The Montezuma.[10] It also burned on August 8, 1885, only four months after reopening.

This one didn't completely decimate the hotel as the previous fire did, but it did necessitate a massive remodel—one less grand than its predecessors. As times changed, business dwindled, and The Montezuma began to die a slow, less fiery-dramatic death until it closed its doors on Halloween night in 1903. "Perhaps there was an old Indian curse on the place," F. Stanley mused in his booklet.

However, The Montezuma continued to operate in diverse ways, first serving as a Baptist College, then later as a seminary for Jesuits from Mexico. Today, it still stands and operates as the Armand Hammer United World College of the American West and has hosted royalty. So, in a strange way, Emperor Montezuma's royal legacy continues. In the words of Stanford in her *True West* article on the beloved hotel:

> Could it be that Chief Montezuma, god of the ancient Pecos Indians, has indeed fulfilled his promise and returned to the land of his people?[11]

Chapter Notes

[1] In *Place Names of New Mexico*, Robert Julyan said the place was so named because of a Pecos legend that Montezuma journeyed there to utilize the spring's healing waters rather than being born there. [pp.232-233]
[2] Stanley, *Montezuma Story*, p.3.
[3] Ibid.
[4] Stanford, "Fabulous Montezuma," *True West*, p.31.
[5] Stanley, *Montezuma Story*, p.4.
[6] Stanford, "Fabulous Montezuma," *True West*, p.30.
[7] Stanley, *Montezuma Story*, p.11.
[8] On the note of dinner, thanks to a train from Mexico, sea turtles were on the menu. Later, during operation, a tank was on grounds to keep live sea turtles to stay on the menu permanently as they were routinely transported on the railroad from Mexico.
[9] Stanley, *Montezuma Story*, p.14.
[10] Some say this monicker was given to the hotel's third iteration rather than the second.
[11] Stanford, "Fabulous Montezuma," *True West*, p.50.

22.

MONTEZUMA AT SIERRA BLANCA
The Great White Bat

Tales of Montezuma in Southeastern New Mexico are decidedly rare. However, there is at least one, though its veracity is debatable at best. The sole source of the story, so far as this author can tell, can only be attributed to the *St. Louis Globe Democrat*, which had a penchant for telling fantastic tales. The *Globe* story, entitled "Legend of the Sierra Blanca: The Mysterious Great White Bat, Who Holds Full Sway There," made the rounds in 1901 and was retrieved in this instance from the *Evening Star* of February 9, 1901.

The story began in northern New Mexico, in the vicinity of what is today the Rinconada Canyon Petroglyph National Monument, in the region near Albuquerque. As with most areas in New Mexico, its history, illustrated by petroglyphs on the rocks, is steeped in the Spanish conquest and the habitation of the Puebloans.

"About seven generations ago," began the 1901 article, a group of cross-wielding, robed Spanish priests accompanied by "strange warriors carrying thunder sticks" entered a village near the Rinconada, "where the inhabitants engraved their story on the rocks." The vague article even implied that Montezuma's eternal flame was located in an estufa near Rinconada rather than Pecos. So the article went,

Rinconada Canyon Petroglyph National Monument.
(NPS Photo/Daniel Leifheit)

The strangers defiled there the sacred estufa, quenched the sacred fire and planted a crossed stick. They murdered all of the priests of the estufa but one, who lay sick in his house. In the middle of the night he who was sick crawled to the estufa, saved some of the live coals, and in his house fanned to life again the sacred fire. At the coming of dawn the [priests] seized the white-haired old priest. The soldiers tied him to the tail of a horse, dragged him through the village and beat him with a whip of bull's hide until he fell to the ground as one dead, and he lay there in the burning sunshine all day, unconscious and without food or water. As he lay thus, there came to him the spirit of Montezuma and whispered unto him: "Take thou the sacred fire to the abode of the great white bat, and there those that suffer for me shall see my face, their hurts be healed and their grievances avenged," and as the rays of the sun came over the Sierra Blanca and the gray mists of dawn were being transformed into banks of gold, ruby and silver, floating high above, there, in the innermost depth of the mountain, was burning the sacred fire.

LEGEND OF THE SIERRA BLANCA.

The Mysterious Great White Bat, Who Holds Full Sway There.

From the St Louis Globe Democrat.

Half way up the Sierra Blanca peak, approaching it from the south, where the cedars and the spruce trees are thickest and the pinon grows in profusion, there is a perpendicular wall of rock. Go eastward to its end, turn around its jagged corner, and there is a narrow shelf rising rapidly several hundred feet and leading to a small, deep canyon, in which there is a very dense growth of trees. Dark is the shade and profuse the growth of ferns and mosses, and velvety under foot the dark soil made of the leaves that have fallen for ages. Go up this small canyon a few hundred yards; then stop and go no farther. Before you is the mouth of a canyon leading to the heart of the Sierra. Its height is equal to the height of three men, and its width is equal to four times its height, and so dense is the growth of trees at its mouth that little, if any, light can enter it. Within is blackness profound. At dusk there emerge from it clouds upon clouds of the winged bats, who return at the early dawn.

Before going any further, it should be stated that southern New Mexico's Sierra Blanca most certainly cannot be seen all the way from northern New Mexico's Rinconada Canyon. But, this being a story told in the not-so-accountable golden age of newspapers, we shall proceed. The beaten priest of the sacred flame trekked, somehow, to Sierra Blanca and entered the abode of the Great White Bat. Hanging within an "immense arched cavern" in the mountain, the paper described the gigantic bat as being "twice as large as the largest buffalo, and each of its wings has the length of ten varas…"

Postcard depicting Sierra Blanca in Lincoln County, New Mexico. The nearby Capitan Mountains also have an Aztec legend associated with them. Similar to the tale of the Taos treasure in Wheeler Peak recounted earlier, the story went that a procession of Aztecs sent by Montezuma hid a treasure cache in a cave in El Capitan. Though the cavern was said to have once been inhabited by a race of fantastical giants, no mention was made of the Great White Bat.

Two priests, accompanied by ten soldiers, trailed the old beaten priest by way of hounds to the mountain. They entered the sacred cavern, which was "100 varas high" and "lost in the blackness of night, they found the aged priest of Montezuma, praying before the sacred fire."

And they rushed forward with evil intent, when, with the roar of the hurricane, there came down from the dome of the cavern, like an arrow shot from a bow, the great white bat, and with one blow of his wings he struck all of them down. Seizing two steel-clad warriors in each claw and one in his mouth, he flew out of the cavern, and the flames of the sacred fire leaped high in salute as he passed. In a few moments he returned, seized five more and flew out, and again he returned, and seizing the two priests of the evil one, whose wails of agony could be heard reechoing through the cavern and its labyrinth of passages, he disappeared for a longer time.

On his return he carried on his back the priests that had been slain in the sacred estufa of the Rinconado. He threw the dogs upon the sacred fire and went to sleep again in the dome of the cavern, awaiting the further summons of his master.

Though not mentioned, it's possible that the creator of this tale drew inspiration for the Great White Bat of Montezuma from the bat deity Camazotz from Mayan mythology.

Following that,

In the village, in the broad light of day, six graves opened, and six priests of Montezuma arose therefrom, mounted an invisible steed and disappeared in the skies.

The strangers and the remaining priest who witnessed this crossed themselves and fled from the village. In the heart of the mountain there is yet burning the sacred fire and guarding it until the return of Montezuma are the seven priests of the Rinconada.

As further proof of the story, the *Globe Democrat* reported that a group of Comanche 100 miles to the south in the Guadalupe Mountains found "the bodies of ten strange warriors, whose armor was shattered into fragments and imbedded in the rotting flesh." The priests were nowhere to be found, and presumably had been devoured by the bat. The article then concluded by revealing the tale was told by a woman simply identified as Mariana, who had heard it from her great-grandfather.

Due to the fantastic nature of the story and its source via the *Globe Democrat*, it's my best guess that a writer with a loose grasp of New Mexico's geography and an understanding of Aztec mythology made the story up, as I have never heard any variation of it elsewhere.

23.

RETURN OF MONTEZUMA
Prophets of Montezuma in Santa Fe

I t's hard to say when the widely held tradition of looking to the dawn light for Montezuma's return began to die out. One of the last gasps of the second coming of Montezuma was reported in various newspapers in 1907. So they said, two prophets of Montezuma were wandering the streets of Santa Fe and preparing for his return. Supposedly, the duo hailed from a mysterious village eighty miles west of Santa Fe known as Huncara.

The village was said to have been founded by a mysterious descendant of the Aztecs, a prophet of Montezuma named Maxtla, who the paper described only as "an aged man who lives a retired life in the mountains to the west of the city."

The article, retrieved from the *San Francisco Bulletin* of July 24, 1907, began

> Awaiting the return of Montezuma, two descendants of the race that once peopled old Mexico are wandering around Santa Fe visiting the conquerors and drawing and drawing pictures of the government that is to be established on the old throne and seeking news of the return of their prince to earth.

AZTECS AWAITING MONTEZUMA'S RETURN

SANTA FE, N. M., July 24.—Awaiting the return of Montezuma, two descendants of the race that once peopled all Mexico are wandering around Santa Fe, visiting the conquerors and drawing and drawing pictures of the government that is to be established on the old throne and seeking news of the return of their prince to earth.

The two do not claim any prophetic vision of their own. They have a vague idea of grandeur. They rely on the wisdom of Maxtla, an aged man who lives a retired life in the mountains to the west of the city. "Maxtla knows." They are but his scouts, come down to the nearest point where information may be obtained of the coming of the king, and ready to carry to Maxtla the news when Montezuma shall appear.

It continued that the two men were camped out in a small tent along "a creek a short distance beyond Santa Fe." Apparently, Maxtla felt that if Montezuma returned, he would first appear at the capital of the territory, Santa Fe. Like in the days of the Pueblo Revolt, the two men were said to be fleet-footed, and thus, if Montezuma returned, they could cross the eighty-mile distance between Santa Fe and Huncara to tell of Montezuma's coming.

The paper reported

> Every day they come with the dawn to haunt the mesa, until about noon; and then return to their small camp. During the afternoon they return to talk with some of the Mexicans residing in the lower part of town.

Postcard depicting the plaza in Santa Fe in the early 1900s.

Eavesdroppers reported that typically the duo spoke in "Mexicanized Spanish" though occasionally they also spoke in a language completely unknown to the listeners, thought to be Aztec. "When asked to explain any sentence in this alien speech the two will chatter together for a moment and then turn their faces toward the questioner without an answer," the paper said.

Only at times do these men deign to impart the slightest information regarding themselves or their mission. In fact, had their errand not been a custom of many years no information regarding it would be obtainable.

These pilgrimages began years ago and are evidently part of the system by which the prophet Maxtla maintains an ascendancy over the minds of his fellows. Just when these annual trips from the Huncara settlement of Aztecs began is not known here, but ten years ago a drunken scout betrayed the secret. The pilgrimages were then a matter of established custom and had been for a long time.

RETURN OF MONTEZUMA.
How the watchers gather at Santa Fe to await the coming of Montezuma, the great king of a once mighty race, will be told in The Sunday Tribune.

Of Montezuma's second coming, the two were known to recount the deeds and the kingdom of the Aztec emperor, stating that his second kingdom would be like the first. However, the duo seemed to have forgotten about the emperor's indulgence in human sacrifice, as it never got a mention:

There comes one who will make himself a throne where the old one stood. The Mexican and the American will not resist him, for he will have power beyond all known. He will be Montezuma. For hundreds of years he has studied in his tomb, planning a way to drive out these men who now hold the country. When he comes his people will gather about him. We may not be many now, but his power will be that of everything. The armies he will want will come to him. They will know him by the sign. When he comes all these foreigners will go away. We will have no railroads, no wires carrying the talk of men. We will be like the children who lived in Montezuma's own time, all good, and true! He will have one big war to make unbelieving people bow to him, and then—no more war. Nothing but happiness, sweet gardens, lovely maidens, brave boys—all good.

Above are pictured historic remains of Jemez Pueblo c.1877 as photographed by John K. Hiller's. Considering that the surviving residents of Pecos migrated to Jemez, and that the mysterious "Aztec settlement" of Huncara, mentioned in the 1907 article, was eighty miles west of Santa Fe, could it have been related in some way to Jemez Pueblo?

The article then went on to speculate about the alleged Aztec colony eighty miles west of Santa Fe, claiming that "small ceremonies" were held and were "modeled after the old customs" but "the ceremony varies that human life is no longer sacrificed." Instead, Maxtla was said to sacrifice animals "and read his messages from their beating heats when exposed to air." The mysterious Maxtla, they presumed, was "descended from some relative of that Maxtla of Montezuma's own time, who was chief of the palace guard."[1]

The article reiterated that not much was known of when Montezuma would return, and what little was divulged occurred ten years ago when one of the previous runners partook of some whiskey which loosened his tongue.

"They come now, year after year, more as if fulfilling some duty imposed upon them than as being buoyed with the hope of hearing wonderful news," the article more or less concluded.

Today, I can find no trace of the mysterious settlement called Huncara west of Santa Fe. Could it have simply been the invention of a deceitful newspaper reporter? However, one very intriguing possibility remains. In surveying what lies roughly 80 miles west of Santa Fe, one can't help but notice Jemez Pueblo. If you'll recall, the last survivors of Pecos Pueblo left their homes in 1838 to go to Jemez, which they shared a common lineage and language with. Could this mysterious "Aztec cult" have come from survivors of Pecos Pueblo in the Jemez region, still awaiting Montezuma's return?[2]

Ultimately, only one thing is for certain; while Montezuma may have never returned to the Southwest as promised, he certainly left his mark on the region.

Chapter Notes

[1] Historically speaking, Maxtla was a Tepanec ruler of Azcapotzalco from 1426 to 1428, when he died.

[2] Tangentially related to the "Aztec cult" eighty miles west of Santa Fe could have been Zia Pueblo, located only twelve miles south of Jemez Pueblo. It should be noted that around the same time that the two "prophets" were frequenting Santa Fe, allegations were brought forth that human sacrifices were occurring at Zia Pueblo in 1906. Specifically, it was said that infants were being fed to a giant rattlesnake as in the days of Pecos Pueblo. Papers of the time specifically linked the practice to the "snake worship" of the Aztecs and reported that the claims were brought forward by a Catholic priest to a grand jury in Albuquerque. Because no evidence of the detestable ritual could be established, the charges against Zia Pueblo were dropped.

APPENDIX I
Montezuma and the Flood

The Philadelphia Inquirer *of November 17, 1869, presented this legend conjoining Montezuma with the Great Flood.*

Before the flood, men lived to a great age so that they lost their teeth and crept about like children. After a time they would get new teeth, and walk upright again like men in the prime of life. Then it was that the Great Spirit created the mountains and peopled the earth on all sides. Then, too, animals talked like men, and were the first to tell of the approaching flood. About this time appeared Montezuma, who collected a large quantity of gum from a plant called *chuchi*, and with this gum, which is wild to be insoluble in water, and with other materials, he built a large vessel, in which he took refuge, closing and sealing the door behind him. In like manner a coyote or prairie dog crept into a large cane stalk and closed the ends against the water. The flood came up to the highest mountains, and reached even the birds, which cried like men with fright. When the waters came down, Montezuma and the coyote landed at Cerro Prietta, which mountain some believe to be Montezuma's vessel.

According to another tradition, they landed in the center of the earth, and, having come out of their vessels, Montezuma noticed the trail of a beetle, which he followed until he found the beetle fast in the mud. He then turned back, and, meeting the coyote, they embraced each other in grief. Montezuma sent the coyote southward to find the sea, which it soon found and returned, when it was sent on the same errand to the northward, but returned unsuccessful. They then lay down to sleep, when Montezuma dreamed that he should form men and women out of clay, which he accordingly did, making two for each nation. Meanwhile, the coyote sat behind him also making men, but the latter were ill-formed, so that Montezuma ordered them to be removed. His own people multiplied rapidly, and built a large city on the north bank of a river, supposed to be at the mouth of Salt river, in Arizona, where the remains of large ditches are still visible.

Montezuma next traveled southward, followed by large numbers of people. In accordance with a dream, he thrust a rod into the earth, and water flowed thence, which is the origin of the springs at Santa Rosa and elsewhere. After a time the Great Spirit appeared to Montezuma as an old man, and asked to baptize the people, that they might live beyond the sky after death, but Montezuma became angry and killed the Great Spirit. Then the latter arose from the dead by night and repeated the request, when Montezuma grew angry again, declared that he would take his people to heaven by a tower, and killed the Great Spirit a second time, leaving him on the ground, where he was dragged about as a plaything for four years. He then returned to Heaven, removing the sun further from the earth as he ascended.

After a long interval he descended again with the same request as before. At this time Montezuma was living at the Casa Blanco, or white house, close to the Pima villages on the Gila river. The inside of this house was overlaid with pure gold. A third time he slew the Great Spirit, but the latter now becoming angry, threw a louse into Spain, which led to an invasion by the Spaniards. Twice did Montezuma meet and repel the invaders, but before the third engagement the golden ring flew from the finger of his daughter to the finger of the Spanish commander, and the silver ring of the latter flew to the finger of the former.

Thus did she become leagued with the enemy, and when they were out of provisions she prevailed upon her people to throw them *tomales* instead of arrows, and thus they were fed at Montezuma's expense. After many severe conflicts the Spaniards were victorious when the traitorous Princess demanded the hand of the commander in marriage, he agreed to this on condition that an eagle which he set free should alight on a prickly pear tree. The eagle did so, and the commander started to celebrate the marriage at the pear tree, being followed by a large train of Papagoes; but, under the pretext of getting violins, powder, etc., he traveled on and on until the Indians all deserted him.

Henceforth, as the story goes, Montezuma made no improvements, and his people were scattered over the country, he afterwards deposited the archives of the Papago and Pimo nations in a cave near Santa Rosa, and ordered that they celebrate the feast there every fourth year, which custom is still observed. The nation gradually diminished, and Montezuma wandered about until the Indians have lost all traces of him.

APPENDIX II
Sacred Tree of Pecos

Here is the full article that was quoted from in chapter seven on the sacred tree of Pecos as it appeared in the El Paso Daily Herald *of November 12, 1900, on page two:*

A PRETTY LEGEND.
It Is Told of the Ruined Indian Pueblo of Pecos.

Marion Hill, in Frank Leslie's Popular Magazine tells the following romantic legend about the ruined pueblo of Pecos, around which so much romance has been woven:

"Through all the grotesque darkness of Pueblo superstition runs a bright thread of poetic legend: and one legend is woven around the ruined estufa in the ruined pueblo of Pecos. Pecos was founded by the man god, the great Montezuma himself, and he therefore probably felt a protective interest in it; at any rate, when the usurping Spaniards lay upon the conquered Pueblos the cursed rule of restraint and wrong. Montezuma invoked against them the aid of his brother gods in heaven. These told him to plant a tree upside down beside the chief estufa of Pecos, and to light a holy fire upon the altar, and if the fire kept burning until the tree fell, then would there come to the rescue of the oppressed a great pale face nation and deliver them from the Spanish thrall.

So the fire was lit and a sentinel was posted to guard its sacred flame; and the tree was planted—under the circumstances the planter would be excusable in planting the tree as insecurely as possible. But year after year passed, and the tree remained standing Sentinel succeeded sentinel and the flame lived on. Generations withered away, yet deliverance seemed no nearer. One day there came a rumor from old Santa Fe that the city had surrendered to a white-faced people. Was this the band of deliverers? That day at noon the sacred tree toppled and fell. Spanish rule was no more. The prophecy had been fulfilled.

"If there he an unbeliever of this legend, let him go to the ruins of Pecos and see for himself that whereas the city was built upon a mesa so barren that no trees are there nor ever have been there, yet across the crumbling estufa lies the fallen body of a pine of mighty growth. The like of it is not for many miles around. "Whence then, did it come?"

BIBLIOGRAPHY

Books

Applegate, Frank G. *Indian Stories from the Pueblos*. Borodino Books (Kindle Edition).

Aragón, Ray John de. *New Mexico Native American Lore: Skinwalkers, Kachinas, Spirits and Dark Omens*. The History Press, 2022.

Arment, Chad. *Boss Snakes: Stories and Sightings of Giant Snakes in North America*. Coachwhip Publications, 2008.

Bancroft, Hubert Howe. *History of Arizona and New Mexico, 1530-1888*. Harvard University, 1889.

Bandelier, Adolph. *A Visit to the Aboriginal Ruins in the Valley of the Rio Pecos*. Archaeological Institute of America, 1881.

Bullock, Alice. *Living Legends Of The Santa Fe Country: A Collection Of Southwestern Stories*. Green Mountain Press, 1970.

------------------ *Mountain Villages*. Sunstone Press, 1973.

Cather, Willa. *Death Comes for the Archbishop*. Alfred A. Knopf, 1927.

Davis, W.W.H. *El Gringo; Or, New Mexico and Her People*. Harper & Brothers, 1857.

Dobie, Frank J. *Coronado's Children: Tales of Lost Mines and Buried Treasure in the Southwest*. University of Texas Press, 1978.

Emory, W.H. *Notes of a Military Reconnaissance, From Fort Leavenworth, in Missouri, to San Diego, in California, Including Part of the Arkansas, Del Norte, and Gila Rivers.* (1848)

Espinoza, J. Manuel. *The Pueblo Indian Revolt of 1696 and the Franciscan Missions in New Mexico: Letters of the Missionaries and Related Documents.* University of Oklahoma Press, 1991.

Gregg, Josiah. *Commerce of the Prairies.* University of Oklahoma Press, 1958.

Hackett, Charles W. and Charmion C. Shelby. *Revolt of the Pueblo Indians of New Mexico and Otermin's Attempted Reconquest, 1680-1682.* University of New Mexico Press, 1970.

Horgan, Paul. *Great River: The Rio Grande in North American History.* Holt, Rinehart and Winston, 1965.

Jaramillo, Cleofas M. *Shadows of the Past.* Ancient City Press, 1972.

Julyan, Robert. *The Place Names of New Mexico: Revised Edition.* University of New Mexico Press, 1998.

Kessell, John L. *Kiva, Cross, & Crown: The Pecos Indians and New Mexico, 1540-1840.* Western National Parks Association, 2014.

Kutz, Jack. *Mysteries and Miracles of New Mexico.* Rhombus Press, 1988.

Lange, Charles H. and Carroll L. Riley (Ed.) *The Southwestern Journals of Adolph F. Bandelier 1883-1884 edited and annotated by Charles H. Lange and Carroll L. Riley.* University of New Mexico Press, 1970.

Lummis, Charles. *A New Mexico David: And Other Stories and Sketches of the Southwest.* Charles Scribner's Sons, 1891.

------------------------*Mesa, Cañon and Pueblo: Our Wonderland of the Southwest, Its Marvels of Nature, Its Pageant of the Earth Building, Its Strange Peoples, Its Centuried Romance.* The Century Co., 1925.

Mayor, Adrienne. *Fossil Legends of the First Americans.* Princeton University Press, 2005.

Parsons, Elsie C. *The Social Organization of the Tewa of New Mexico.* Kraus, 1974.

Penfield, Thomas. *Dig Here! Lost Mines & Buried Treasure of the Southwest.* Adventures Unlimited Press, 1962/2004.

Porter, Clyde and Mae Reed (Compilers). John E. Sunder (Editor). *Matt Field on the Santa Fe Trail.* University of Oklahoma Press, 1960.

Robinson, Sherry. *Apache Voices: Their Stories of Survival as Told to Eve Ball.* University of New Mexico Press, 2000.

Schroeder, Albert & Homer Hastings. *Montezuma Castle.* (1961)

Simmons, Marc. *Witchcraft in the Southwest: Spanish and Indian Supernaturalism on the Rio Grande.* Bison Books, Kindle Edition.

Sonderman, Joe. *Route 66 in New Mexico.* Arcadia Publishing, 2010.

Stanely, F. *The Montezuma, New Mexico Story.* By the author, 1963.

Stansfield, Charles. *Haunted Arizona.* Globe Pequot, 2020.

Steiger, Brad and Sherry Hansen-Steiger. *Montezuma's Serpent and Other Supernatural Tales of the Southwest.* Paragon House, 1992.

Articles

Bandelier, Adolph. "The "'Montezuma' of the Pueblo Indians." *American Anthropologist* (Vol. 5. October 1892).

Beninato, Stefanie. "Popé, Pose-yemu, and Naranjo: A New Look at Leadership in the Pueblo Revolt of 1680." *New Mexico Historical Review* (Vol. 65, #4, 1990).
https://digitalrepository.unm.edu/nmhr/vol65/iss4/2

Chavez, Fray Angelico. "Pohé-yemo's Representative and the Pueblo Revolt." *New Mexico Historical Review* (Vol. 42, #2, April 1967).

Espinosa, Aurelio M. "New-Mexican Spanish Folk-Lore" *The Journal of American Folklore* Vol. 23, No. 90 (Oct. - Dec., 1910)

Howe, Carl. "Did the Dutchman find Montezuma's Treasure?" *Gold!* (Almanac, 1969).

Mason, J. Alden. "The Papago Migration Legend." *Journal of American Folklore* (Vol. 34, No. 133, Jul.-Sep., 1921)

Stanford, Pearl. "Fabulous Montezuma." *True West* (July/August 1967).

INDEX

ABOUT THE AUTHOR

John LeMay was born and raised in Roswell, NM, the "UFO Capital of the World." He is the author of over 50 books, many of them on the history of the Southwest such as *Tall Tales and Half Truths of Billy the Kid,* and *Roswell USA: Towns That Celebrate UFOs, Lake Monsters, Bigfoot and Other Weirdness.* In addition to non-fiction, he is also the author of the novels *The Noted Desperado Pancho Dumez* and *Once Upon a Time in Fort Sumner.* He is also the editor/publisher of *Strange West Magazine* and has written for Western journals and magazines such as *True West, The Coalition Journal,* the *Tombstone Epitaph,* and the *Wild West History Association Journal.* He is a Past President of the Board of Directors for the Historical Society for Southeast New Mexico.

The following titles are available for purchase on Amazon.com, and are available to bookstores at a wholesale discount via Ingram Content Group (ISBNs of available editions listed for this purpose)

CRYPTOZOOLOGY/COWBOYS & SAURIANS

Cowboys & Saurians: Prehistoric Beasts as Seen by the Pioneers explores dinosaur sightings from the pioneer period via real newspaper reports from the time. Well-known cases like the Tombstone Thunderbird are covered along with more obscure cases like the Crosswicks Monster and more. Softcover (357 pp/5.06" X 7.8") Suggested Retail: $19.95 ISBN: 978-1-7341546-1-0

Cowboys & Saurians: Ice Age zeroes in on snowbound saurians like the Cerato-saurus of the Arctic Circle and a Tyrannosaurus of the Tundra, as well as sightings of Ice Age megafauna like mammoths, glyptodonts, Sarkastodons and Saber-toothed tigers. Tales of a land that time forgot in the Arctic are also covered. Softcover (264 pp/5.06" X 7.8") Suggested Retail: $14.99 ISBN: 978-1-7341546-7-2

Southerners & Saurians takes the series formula of exploring newspaper accounts of monsters in the pioneer period with an eye to the Old South. In addition to dinosaurs are covered Lizardmen, Frogmen, giant leeches and mosquitoes, and the Dingocroc, which might be an alien rather than a prehistoric survivor. Softcover (202 pp/5.06" X 7.8") Suggested Retail: $13.99 ISBN: 978-1-7344730-4-9

Cowboys & Saurians South of the Border explores the saurians of Central and South America, like the Patagonian Plesiosaurus that was really a lemisch, plus tales of the Neo-Mylodon, a menacing monster from underground called the Minhocao, Glyptoconts, and even Bolivia's three-headed dinosaur! Softcover (412 pp/ 5.06"X7.8") Suggested Retail: $17.95 ISBN: 978-1-953221-73-5

UFOLOGY/THE REAL COWBOYS & ALIENS IN CONJUNCTION WITH ROSWELL BOOKS

The Real Cowboys and Aliens: Early American UFOs explores UFO sightings in the USA between the years 1800-1864. Stories of encounters sometimes involved famous figures in U.S. history such as Lewis and Clark, and Thomas Jefferson. Hardcover (242pp/6" X 9") Softcover (262 pp/5.06" X 7.8") Suggested Retail: $24.99 (hc)/$15.95(sc) ISBN: 978-1-7341546-8-9(hc)/978-1-7344 730-8-7(sc)

The second entry in the series, *Old West UFOs*, covers reports spanning the years 1865-1895. Includes tales of Men in Black, Reptilians, Spring-Heeled Jack, Sasquatch from space, and other alien beings, in addition to the UFOs and airships. Hardcover (276 pp/6" X 9") Softcover (308 pp/5.06" X 7.8") Suggested Retail: $29.95 (hc)/$17.95(sc) ISBN: 978-1-7344730-0-1 (hc)/ 978-1-73447 30-2-5 (sc)

The third entry in the series, *The Coming of the Airships*, encompasses a short time frame with an incredibly high concentration of airship sightings between 1896-1899. The famous Aurora, Texas, UFO crash of 1897 is covered in depth along with many others. Hardcover (196 pp/6" X 9") Softcover (222 pp/5.06" X 7.8") Suggested Retail: $24.99 (hc)/$15.95(sc) ISBN: 978-1-7347816 -1-8 (hc)/978-1-7347816-0-1(sc)

Featuring cases the authors missed, *The Lost Cases* covers things such as the skyquakes recorded by Lewis and Clark, airships and the Spanish American War, Pancho Villa and crystal skulls, lost alien tribe of the Tundra, invisible alien monsters, the Great Moon Hoax of 1835, hellhounds and airships, the Sonora Airship Club and more. Softcover (252 pp/5.06" X 7.8") Suggested Retail: $18.99 ISBN: 978-1-953221-55-1

Cowboys & Saurians: Dinosaurs Down Under takes the series to Australia to explore tales of the cattle devouring Burrunjor, the dreaded Diprotodon, the terrible Tantanoola Tiger, the marsupial Sasquatch known as the Yowie, plus Thylacines, Bunyips, giant rabbits, Megalodons and dinosaurs in nearby New Zealand. Softcover (240 pp/ 5.06" X 7.8") Suggested Retail: $14.95 ISBN: 978-1-953221-34-6

As the title suggest, *Cowboys & Saurians in the Modern Era* takes the series into the 20th Century with tales of the Texas Pterosaur flap of 1976, the Bladenboro Beast of the 1950s, the Busco Turtle Beast of the 1940s, dinosaur sightings in the Great Depression and far out tales of mini-mastodons, dinosaur men, and Snallygasters. Softcover (320 pp/ 5.06" X 7.8") Suggested Retail: $19.95 ISBN: 978-1-953221-22-3

Settlers & Serpents wrangles the best "Snaik Stories" of the Southwest and beyond in a single volume. Whether it's simple giant snakes or lake serpents, they're corralled in the pages within. Also included are entries on the Leviathan in Mesoamerica and the Southwest plus a detailed look at the giant rattlesnake of Pecos Pueblo. Softcover (180 pp/ 5.06" X 7.8") Suggested Retail: $14.99 ISBN: 978-1-953221-21-6

Written for young readers ages 9-12, *Monsters of the Old South* collects the best creature stories of the White River Monster, Green Eyes, the Crocodingo, the Averasboro Gallinipper, the Tennessee Snake Woman, the Arkansas Gowrow, Bigfoot in the Mississippi River and more. Softcover (122 pp/4.25" X 7") Suggested Retail: $12.99 ISBN: 978-17347816-9-4

Early 20th Century UFOs kicks off a new series that investigates UFO sightings of the early 1900s. Includes tales of UFOs sighted over the *Titanic* as it sunk, Nikola Tesla receiving messages from the stars, an alien being found encased in ice, and a possible virus from outer space!!Hardcover (196 pp/6" X 9") Softcover (222 pp/5.06" X 7.8") Suggested Retail: $27.99 (hc)/$16.95(sc) ISBN: 978-1-7347816-1-8 (hc)/978-1-73478 16-0-1(sc)

UFOs in the Roaring Twenties takes a look at UFO sightings in the 1920s just as the title suggests, along with accounts of Mothman in Nebraska, Lincoln LaPaz's first UFO case, Men in Black investigating an airship crash in Braxton County, West Virginia, Camden's Cosmic Sniper, and much more! Softcover (248 pp/5.06" X 7.8") Suggested Retail: $19.99 ISBN: 978-1-953221-51-3

UFOs of the Turbulent Thirties concludes the authors' investigation of the last unexplored decade of Ufology in the Great Depression with accounts of Mothman, Ghost Fliers, Nazi Bells, the Underground City of the Lizard People, a vanished village on the tundra, and even gangsters and aliens. Softcover (212 pp/5.06" X 7.8") Suggested Retail: $17.95 ISBN: 978-1-953221-35-3

Written for young readers ages 9-12, *Space Monsters of the Old West* collects the best alien sightings of the Wild West including Mummies from Mars, Bigfoot from the Moon, Pascagoula's space ghouls, the Crawfordsville Monster, Spring-Heeled Jack, Blobs from space, and even the dinosaurian alien creatures that invaded Van Meter, Iowa. Softcover (120 pp/4.25" X 7") Suggested Retail: $12.99 ISBN: 978-1-953221-87-2

COWBOYS & MONSTERS

Cowboys & Monsters features potentially true stories of real vampires, werewolves, and even mummies unique to America's Wild West period. Examples include the cursed mummy of John Wilkes Booth, New Orleans immortal vampire Jacques St. Germain, precursors to the Beast of Bray Road, and the origins of Skinwalker Ranch. Softcover (316 pp/5.06" X 7.8") Suggested Retail: $19.99 ISBN: 978-1-953221-46-9

The first entry in this trilogy of non-fiction terror sinks its teeth into the lore of the vampire in North America and Mexico, with detailed rundowns on the vampire hunters of Exeter, Rhode Island, a tribe of Bat People, the nocturnal shape-shifting vampire witches of Tlaxcala, the immortal ways of Comte St. Germain in New Orleans and more. Softcover (200 pp/ 5.06" X 7.8") Suggested Retail: $12.99 ISBN: 978-4-953221-38-4

Mummies of the Americas explores Death Valley's city of the Dead, King Tut's Tomb along the Arkansas, the Egyptian City of the Grand Canyon plus the famous mummies of John Wilkes Boothe, Elmer McCurdy, the Cardiff Giant, the Mummy of Helldorado, and even Billy the Kid's pickled trigger finger! Softcover (200 pp/5.06" X 7.8") Suggested Retail: $12.99 ISBN: 978-1-953221-37-7

Cowboys & Dogmen is devoted to tales of werewolves of the Wild West including the dreaded Navajo skinwalker, the Watrous Werewolf, the Beast of the Land Between Lakes, the Hellhounds of El Dorado Canyon, the dreaded Dog Eater, the Wahhoo, the Wolf Man of Versailles, the Michigan Dog-Man and more! Softcover (212 pp/5.06" X 7.8") Suggested Retail: $12.99 ISBN: 978-1-953221-36-0

FICTION/ MISC. HISTORY

The first novel from historian John LeMay weaves a fantastic web of fiction via real life mysteries and legends of New Mexico, namely the puzzling theft and return of Billy the Kid's tombstone in 1976, the legend of the Lost Adams Diggings, the villainous Santa Fe Ring, and the enigmatic Acoma Mesa. Softcover (250 pp/5.5" X 7.5") Suggested Retail: $14.95 ISBN: 978-1-953221-42-1

The year is 1950, and old timers connected to the long-dead outlaw Billy the Kid are turning up murdered in New Mexico. Some blame the killings on the avenging witch of the Navajo nation, the skinwalker, while others think it's no coincidence that a man claiming to be a surviving Billy the Kid is set to meet with the governor soon... Softcover (260 pp/5.5" X 7.5") Suggested Retail: $16.95 ISBN: 978-1-953221-32-2

Roswell, USA, the long-forgotten debut work of John LeMay, is available again and covers the minutia of the infamous Roswell UFO Crash of 1947. Notable chapters include tales of an alien ghost haunting the old airbase, monsters in the nearby Bottomless Lakes, and even a dinosaur sighting outside of town. Softcover (248 pp/6" X 9") Suggested Retail: $14.95 ISBN: 978-0-9817597-5-3

This biography, for the first time ever, tells the history of western journalist Ash Upson, who ghostwrote Pat Garrett's *The Authentic Life of Billy the Kid* in 1882 and also reproduces many of Upson's letters that detailed the harsh realities of frontier life in New Mexico during the turbulent Lincoln County War. Softcover (318 pp/5.5" X 8.5") Suggested Retail: $16.99 ISBN: 978-1953221919

185

THE NEW MEXICO BOOK OF
WITCHES

JOHN LEMAY